YOUTH BIBLE LESSONS

LEVEL 1

LESSON 1

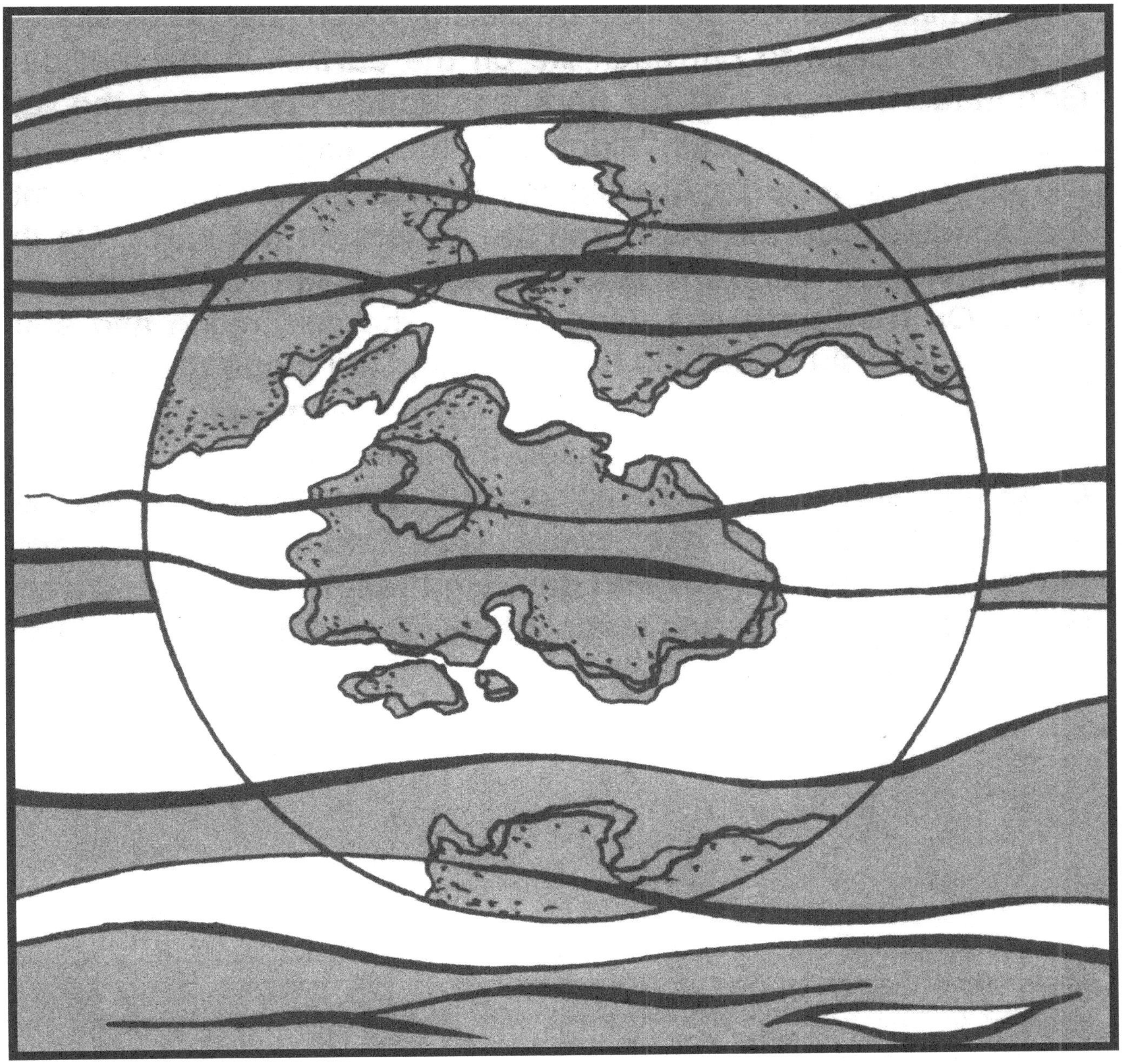

Creation

CREATION

God made the world in the beginning. Much later, God worked for six days to put back life on the earth. On the first day, God made the light and the darkness appear. He called the light "day" and the darkness "night." On the second day, God made the air we breathe by dividing the waters around the earth into the clouds above the earth and the waters on the earth. On the third day, God made the land and seas appear, and plants and trees. On the fourth day, God caused the sun, moon and stars to give their light again. On the fifth day, God made the birds and sea animals. Now everything was ready for man to be able to live. On the sixth day, God made the land animals and man. He could not have made man any sooner because man needs air, light, food, water and heat to live. Now God's physical creation was finished. On the seventh day, God rested from all his work. God blessed this day and made it holy. This is the same Sabbath that we keep each week.

Parents: After reading this story to your child, you may wish to explain, in simple terms, that this was a re-creation. There was a time gap between Genesis 1:1 and 1:2, which is confirmed by passages such as Isaiah 45:18. Prompt discussions with questions such as: What are some of the land animals God made? What kinds of birds do you know? what sea animals can you name?

Day and night

Parents: Instruct your child to cut out pictures from a magazine showing the daytime, with other pictures showing the night. Paste the pictures on this page.

Air we breathe

Parents: Have your child color the pictures. Discuss why air is needed.

Trees God made

Parents: Have your child color the pictures. Discuss the kinds of trees God made. Ask your child the following questions. What plants can you name? Why did God need to make land? What kinds of plants can you eat?

Sun, moon and stars

Parents: Have your child color the picture. Ask him or her the following questions. When do the stars come out? When do the sun and moon appear? Why did God make these things?

Birds

Parents: Have your child color the pictures. Ask him or her the following questions. What are the names of these birds that God made? What other kinds of birds did he create?

Sea animals

Parents: Have your child color the pictures. Ask him or her the following questions. What are the names of these sea animals God made? What are some of the other sea animals that you can name? Which **sea** animals are very small and which are very big?

Land animals

Parents: Have your child color the pictures. Ask him or her the following questions. What are the names of these animals? What other land animals did God make?

The Sabbath

Parents: Instruct your child to cut out pictures from a magazine, newspaper, or from something to be printed from the internet, showing people resting, and paste the pictures above. Discuss this special day that God set aside as a day of rest. Talk about specific ways we are to observe the Sabbath-in addition to resting.

What is this animal?

Parents: Ask your child the following questions. On which day of the first week did God make this animal? What is its name? Are people more important to God than animals?

Connect the dots, then help the chick out of the egg.

YOUTH BIBLE LESSONS

LEVEL 1

LESSON

ADAM AND EVE

God put the first man, Adam, in a beautiful garden called Eden. He told Adam to keep it looking pretty. God told Adam to name all the animals he had made. After Adam named all the animals he was still lonely. He had no one to talk to.

So God made Adam go into a deep sleep. While he was asleep God took one of Adam's ribs and made a woman from it. He called her Eve. Now Adam had a wife and someone to talk to.

God made two special trees in the garden. One was called the Tree of Life and the other was called the Tree of the Knowledge of Good and Evil. God told Adam if he ate of the Tree of Life he could live forever. The only tree God told Adam not to eat of was the Tree of the Knowledge of Good and Evil. God told Adam if he ate of this tree he would die. This didn't mean he would die right then, but that he wouldn't live forever. But Satan came along and told Eve that God had lied. He said they wouldn't really die if they ate of the Tree of Knowledge of Good and Evil. He said they would be like God, able to know right from wrong. But Satan lied.

From that time on, Satan has made people think wrong is right and right is wrong. When Adam and Eve ate of the Tree of the Knowledge of Good and Evil, God knew they would be unhappy. He told them that they would have to leave the beautiful Garden. Now they would have to work hard for their food. God put angels and a flaming sword at the Garden gate so Adam and Eve could not come back. He did not want them to eat of the Tree of Life and live forever in unhappiness believing those wrong thoughts that Satan had put in their minds.

Parents: After reading this to your child you may want to prompt a discussion with some of these questions: Which tree did God tell Adam and Eve not to eat from? Did God mean they would die the minute they ate of the tree? Did Satan tell the truth? What lie did Satan tell Adam and Eve? What tree should they have eaten of? Why did God have to drive them out of the Garden?

Adam and Eve lived in the Garden.

Parents: Explain that even though Adam had all the animals around him, he was still lonely. So God made a woman he could talk to and be his wife.

Adam named all the animals.

Parents: Have your child color the picture of Adam naming the animals. Explain that the names we know the animals as today are not the names Adam originally gave them, because he spoke a different language.

One of the animals Adam named was a duck.

Parents: Ask your child if ducks are clean to eat. What sound does a duck make? Where do they live?

Color the bee and the goat.

Parents: Ask your child what foods we get from each animal. What sounds do they make?

This animal is called a squirrel.
He eats acorns.

Parents: Ask your child these questions: For which season does a squirrel store food? What color fur does a squirrel have? Where do squirrels live?

Adam gave these animals names, too.

Parents: Ask your child to identify these animals. Where do they live? What do they eat?

ANTELOPE

DEER

CHEETAH

Adam also named the antelope, cheetah and deer.

Parents: Ask your child where these animals live. Which of these animals are very fast? Which is the fastest?

Color the giraffe and the hippo.

Parents: Ask your child these questions: How tall are giraffes? How do they drink? Are they clean to eat?

Originally published by the Worldwide Church of God
Produced in cooperation with Imperial Schools
Copyright© 1981. Reprint by *Continuing* Church of God • www.ccog.org

BIBLE MEMORY
Books of the Old Testament

1. Genesis
2. Exodus
3. Leviticus
4. Numbers
5. Deuteronomy
6. Joshua
7. Judges
8. Ruth
9. I Samuel
10. II Samuel
11. I Kings
12. II Kings
13. I Chronicles
14. II Chronicles

Color the seal.

YOUTH BIBLE LESSONS

LEVEL 1

LESSON 3

Cain & Abel

CAIN AND ABEL

Adam and Eve had two boys. One was named Cain, and the other was named Abel. Cain grew up to be a farmer, and Abel grew up to be a shepherd.

In those days people gave offerings to God in a different way than we do today. Abel gave his best little lamb as an offering, and God was pleased with his offering. Cain also had sheep he could have offered, but instead he gave an offering of some of his vegetables.

God was not pleased with Cain's offering, because Cain's attitude was wrong. Cain was jealous and became very angry with Abel because God was pleased with Abel's offering but was not pleased with his offering. So Cain killed Abel.

When God asked Cain where his brother Abel was, Cain lied, saying he didn't know. Cain should have known that God would know what he did, because God sees everything we do.

God was angry with Cain and told him he would have to leave his father and mother and go live by himself with only his wife. Cain must have felt very much like his mother and father had when God sent them out from the Garden of Eden. Now Cain was very lonely.

Parents: Discuss these questions with your child: What is a shepherd? How did Cain and Abel give offerings? Why was Cain's attitude wrong? What commandments did Cain break? Why did God send Cain away?

Adam and Eve had two sons named Cain and Abel.

Abel was a shepherd.

Parents: Discuss what benefits we receive from sheep (clothing, meat, pets).

Cain was a farmer.

Parents: Ask your child what it takes to make plants grow (air, water, sunlight, heat, soil).

Cain and Abel each gave offerings to God.

Jealous Cain killed his brother Abel.

Parents: Explain that even if we hate our brother or friend, it's very bad too (Matthew 5:21-22).

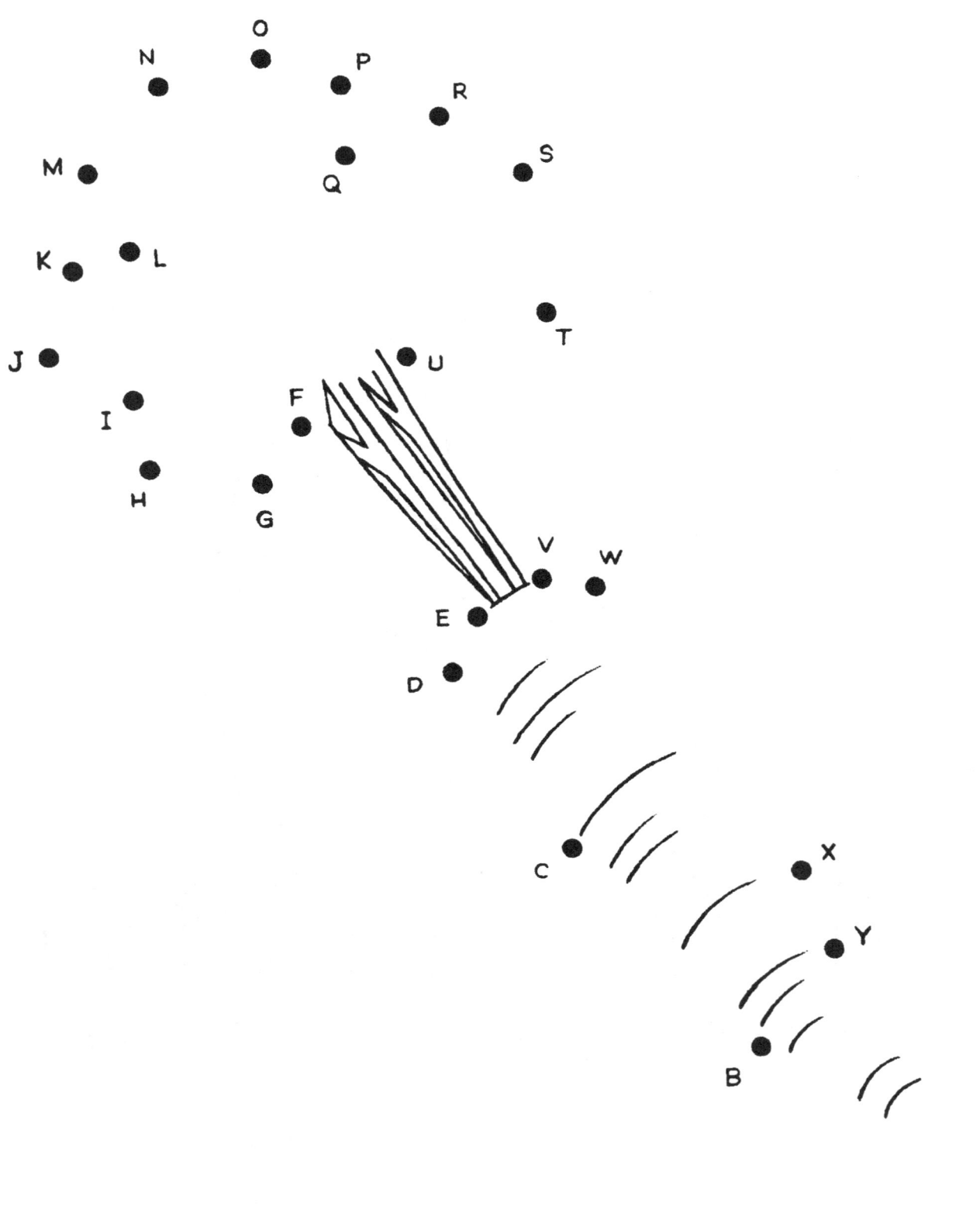

Parents: Have your child connect the letters to see something Cain grew.

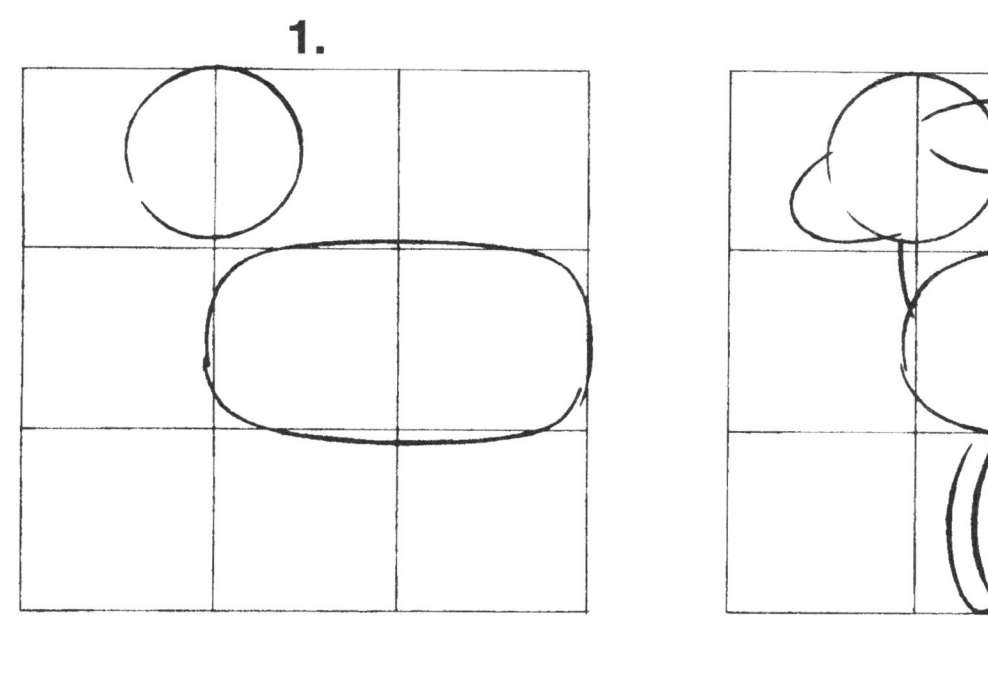

Parents: Your child can practice these drawings on a separate sheet of paper.

CAIN AND ABEL

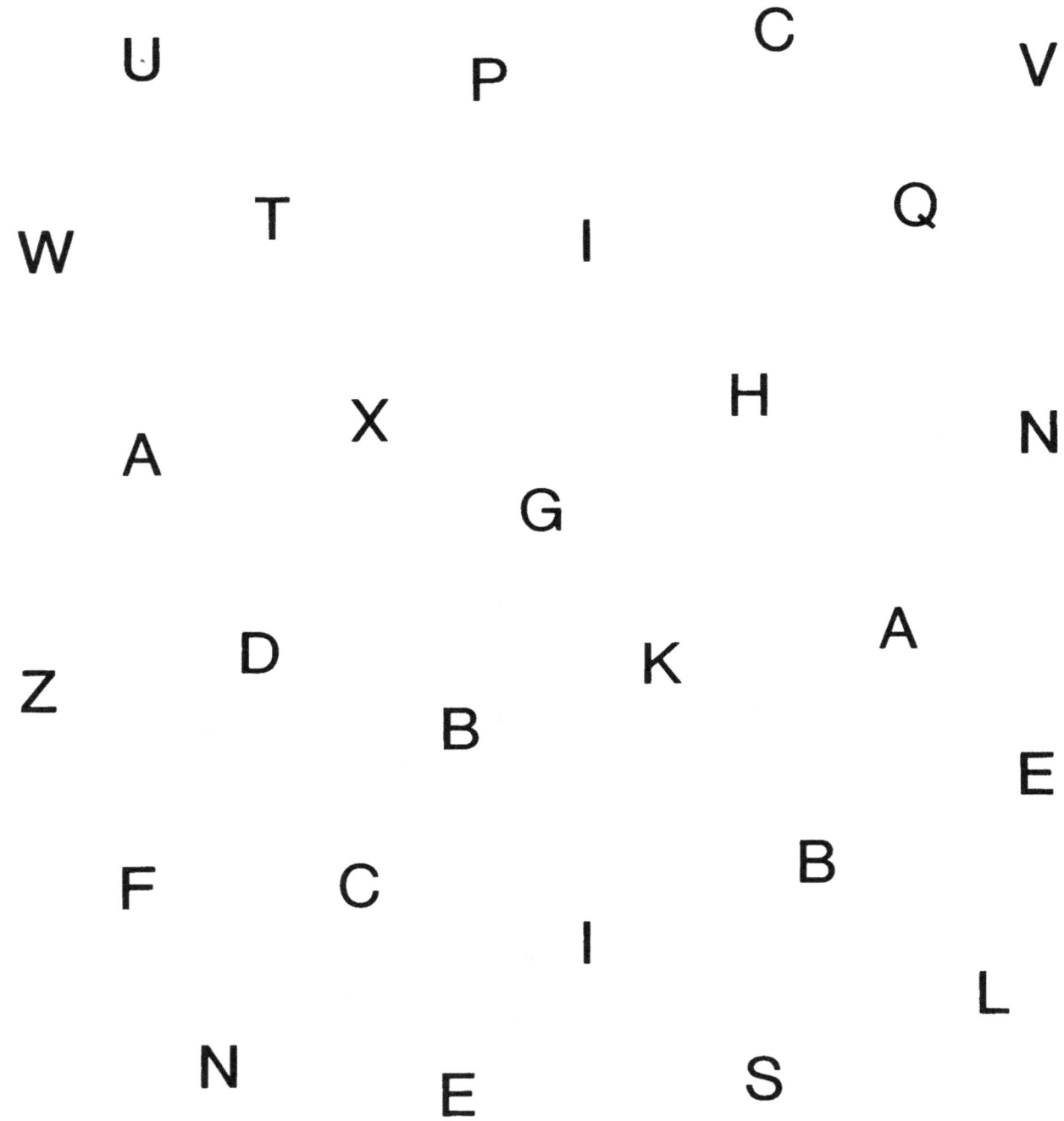

Parents: Instruct your child to circle the letters above that spell these two names: CAIN/ABEL.

Sheep	Shop	Sheep	SHEEP	Shep
Cain	Come	came	Cain	Can
Abel	abel	apple	Abe	Abel
lied	line	dial	lied	lint
lamb	lamp	pam	land	lamb
Adam	Adam	add	And	made
offering	off	ring	offering	over
Eve	even	Eve	Every	elf

Parents: Instruct your child to circle the word that is the same as the one in the box at the left.

Originally published by the Worldwide Church of God
Produced in cooperation with Imperial Schools
Copyright© 1981. Reprint by *Continuing* Church of God • www.ccog.org

BIBLE MEMORY
Books of the
Old Testament
(continued)

15. Ezra
16. Nehemiah
17. Esther
18. Job
19. Psalms
20. Proverbs
21. Ecclesiastes
22. Song of Solomon
23. Isaiah
24. Jeremiah
25. Lamentations
26. Ezekiel
27. Daniel

WHICH WORD DOESN'T BELONG?

1. Adam   Cain   Moses   Eve   Abel

2. lamb   vegetables   sacrifice   offering   tree

3. kill   jealous   hate   love   murder

4. shepherd dog   farmer   keeper of sheep

Parents: As you read these words aloud, have your child underline the one in each row that doesn't fit.

1. Moses   2. tree   3. love   4. farmer

YOUTH BIBLE LESSONS

LEVEL 1

LESSON 4

Noah and the Flood

NOAH AND THE FLOOD

God looked down on the earth and saw all the evil that men were doing. He saw how unhappy this was making them. Therefore God decided to destroy all human beings and all living things on the earth in a great flood. Then He remembered Noah, the only man who obeyed Him. So God told Noah to build a big ark, or ship, out of gopher wood so he, his wife, their three sons and their wives could be saved from the Flood. Noah was told to take seven pairs of each clean animal and bird and one pair of each unclean animal and bird into the ark.

After Noah finished building and loading the ark the rain came. It rained for 40 days and 40 nights. The ark floated for 150 days. Then the water began to go down. When the ark finally came to rest on a mountaintop, Noah sent out a dove. The first time it returned with nothing. Seven days later Noah sent the dove out again. This time it returned with an olive leaf in its beak. After seven more days, the dove was sent out and didn't return. Noah was very happy when the dove didn't return. This meant there was dry land and trees and plants were growing again.

Noah and his family came out of the ark and he built an altar

Parents: Explain to your child what evil is. Explain that God didn't want men to keep on living in terrible unhappiness caused by their disobedience to God. He planned to resurrect them in the Great White Throne Judgment when they will learn God's happy way of life. Explain that "clean" animals are the ones that God created for man to eat. Briefly explain clean and unclean meats.

to give a thank offering to God. God then put a rainbow in the sky. It was a sign to Noah of His promise that He would never again send a flood to destroy everything.

Noah planted a vineyard and grew grapes for wine. Noah was 950 years old when he died.

The ark was made of gopher wood.

Parents: Have your child color the picture of the ark, as well as all the other pictures. Explain to your child how big the ark was in order to hold so many different animals plus enough food for everyone.

God brings the animals to the ark.

Parents: Explain that God told Noah to take more clean animals into the ark because Noah and his family would need some of them for food.

These animals are clean to eat.

Parents: Explain what makes these animals good to eat.

42

God tells us not to eat these unclean animals.

Parents: Explain why these animals are not good to eat.

The dove returns with an olive leaf.

Parents: Explain what it meant when the dove returned with a leaf in its beak.

The rainbow was a sign from God.

Parents: Explain what the rainbow reminds us of.

Noah offers thanks to God for His protection from the Flood.

Parents: Explain how we give offerings today.

Connect the dots to find out how Noah and his family were saved.

BIBLE MEMORY
Books of the
Old Testament
(continued)

28. Hosea
29. Joel
30. Amos
31. Obadiah
32. Jonah
33. Micah
34. Nahum
35. Habakkuk
36. Zephaniah
37. Haggai
38. Zechariah
39. Malachi

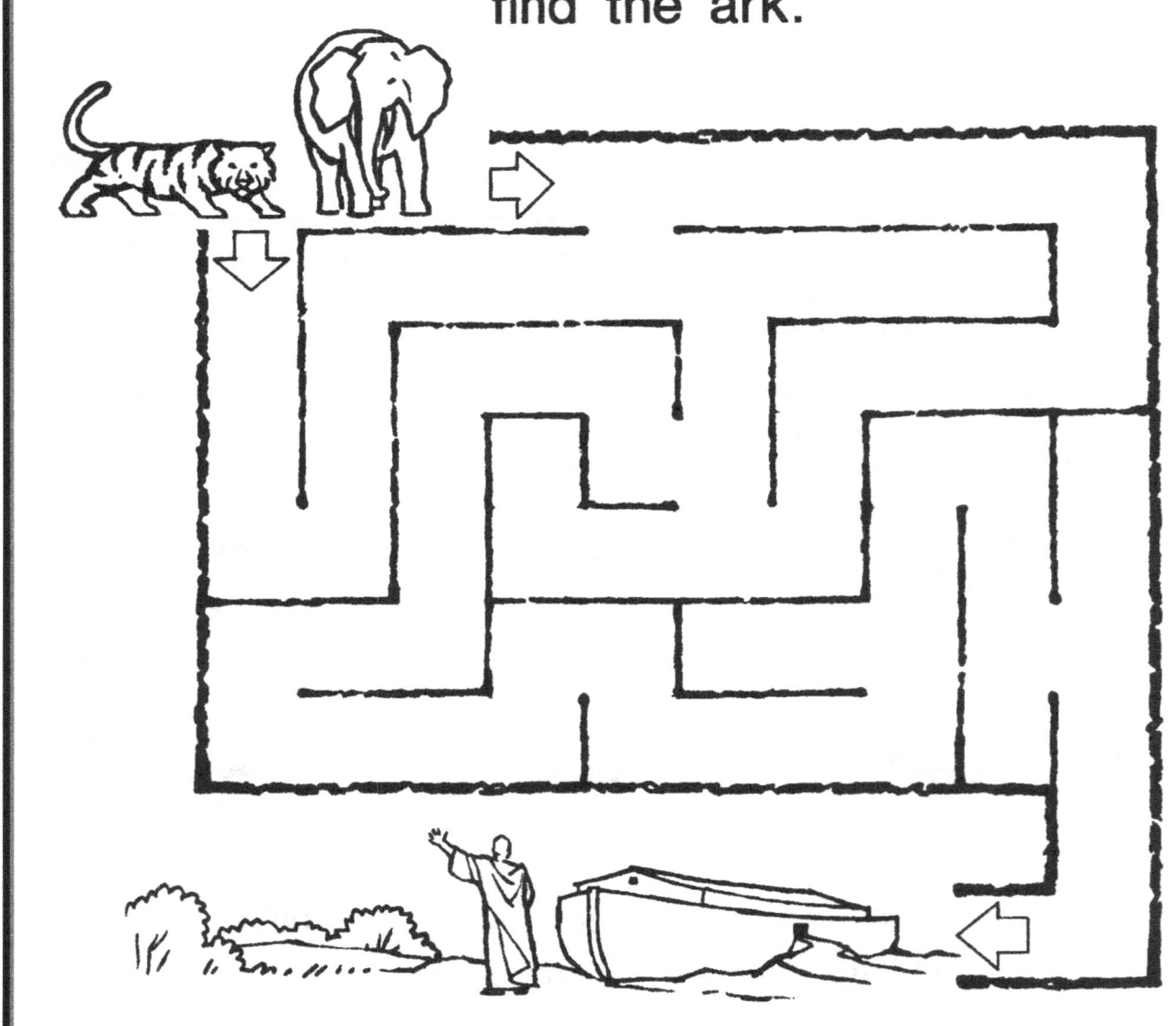

Complete the maze to help the animals find the ark.

YOUTH BIBLE LESSONS

LEVEL 1

LESSON 5

Nimrod and the Tower of Babel

NIMROD AND THE TOWER OF BABEL

The last lesson ended with eight people leaving the ark to start a new life. They were Noah and his wife, his sons Shem, Ham and Japheth and their wives. All the people born after the Flood came from these eight.

One of Noah's three sons, Ham, had a son named Cush. Cush grew up and had a son named Nimrod. This made Nimrod the great grandson of Noah. By this time there were many people on the earth. Most of them settled in a place called Shinar.

Nimrod grew up to be a very strong man and a mighty hunter. People began to look to him as their leader because he was able to protect them from wild animals that attacked them. They began to think of him as a hero. Nimrod liked this.

But Nimrod did not obey God's laws. He wanted the people to look to him, instead of God, as their ruler. He taught them to honor Satan by worshipping things like the sun and snakes. The people liked this. They wanted to worship things they could see and touch. During this time Noah was still alive and telling the people they should obey God. But most of the people would not listen to him.

Since Nimrod wanted the people to follow and obey him, he decided to organize and lead them in building a very tall tower. The tower was to be a temple in honor of the sun, and a symbol of rebellion against God. Since all the people spoke the same language, it was easy for them to work together in building the tower.

The people worked very hard. The tower began to take shape. It became the most important thing in their lives.

God saw what Nimrod and the people were doing. He was not pleased. He had wanted them to spread out after the Flood and live in different parts of the world. He also wanted them to obey His laws. God knew that if the people were allowed to continue following Nimrod in building the tower, they would soon be just as evil and wicked as people were before the Flood.

So God caused the people to suddenly begin speaking different languages. Confusion was the result. Because the people could no longer understand each other, work on the tower came to a stop.

Have you ever tried to talk with someone who doesn't speak your language? If you have, then you know the people could not have worked together and finished the tower.

People soon found others who spoke the same language as they did. They formed small groups and moved away from the city and settled in different places around the world.

Because of the confusion caused by the different languages, the city where they were building the tower was called **Babel**, which means **confusion**. And the tower they never finished building was known from that time on as the Tower of Babel.

Interestingly, even ancient Chinese characters have information about the Flood and the Tower of Babel, which shows that their Ancestors knew about these events.

Nimrod was a strong man and a mighty hunter. He protected the people from wild animals.

Nimrod taught the people to worship the sun and idols in place of God.

Nimrod led the people to build a tower, which was a symbol of their rebellion against God.

God confused the people's language. This stopped work on the tower.

The people began to leave
the city and settle in different
places around the world.

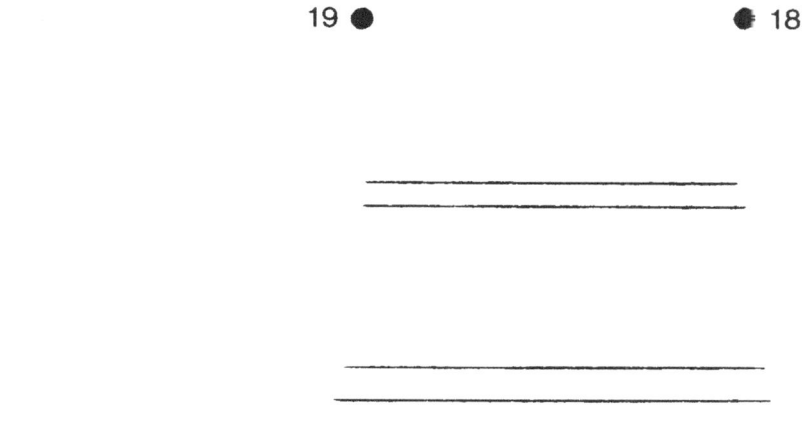
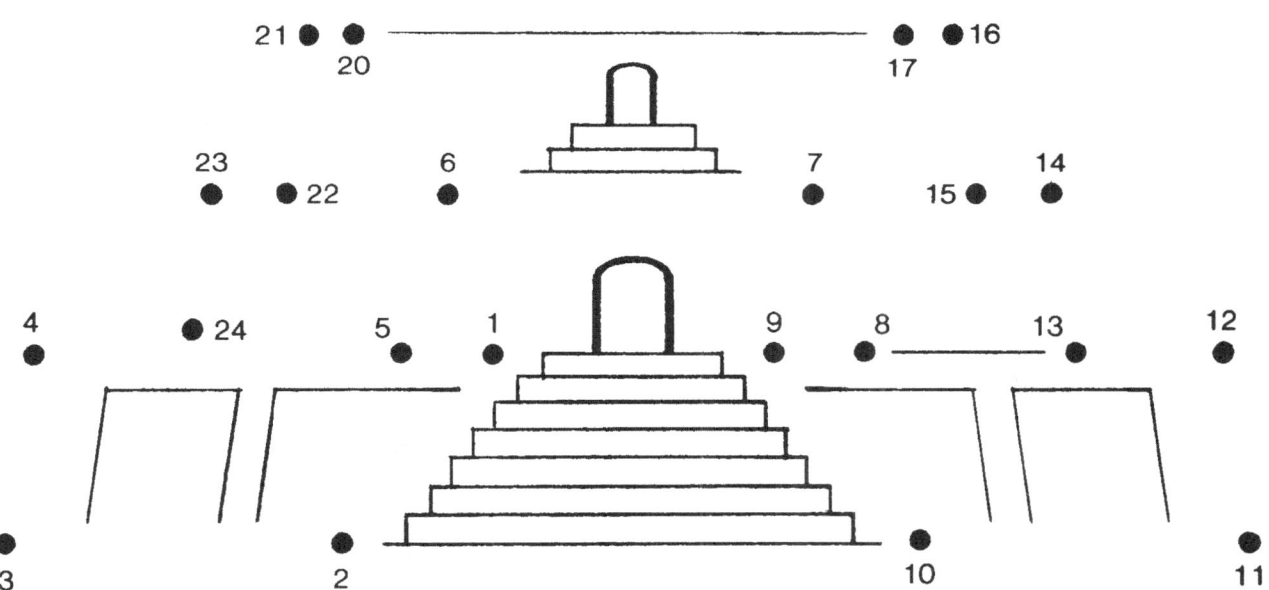

Connect the dots.
See what the people of Babel
started but never finished.

Mixed-up picture

Parents: Have your child cut out the pieces of the picture along the black lines. Arrange the pieces correctly on another piece of paper and paste them down. Then color the picture.

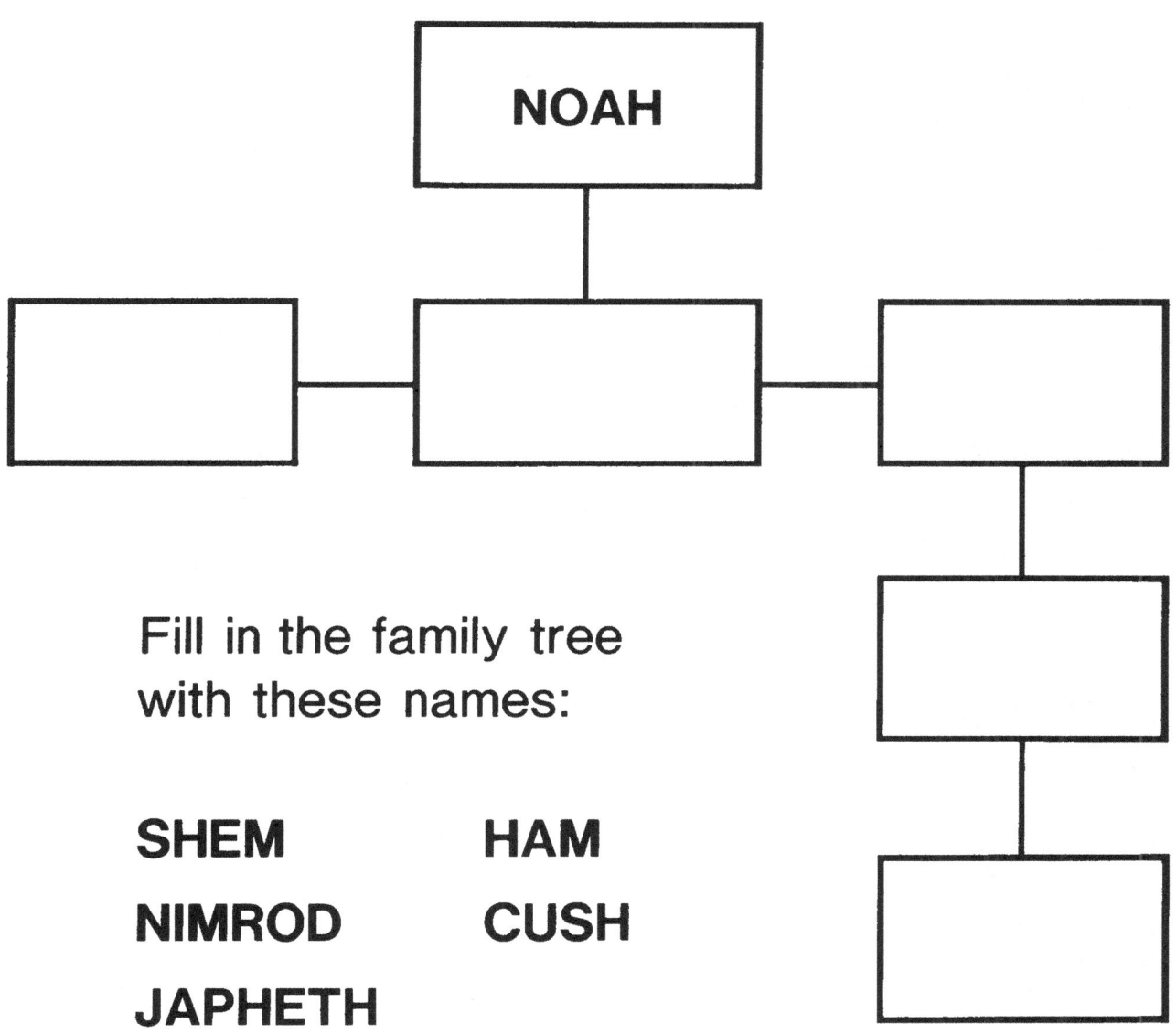

Fill in the family tree with these names:

SHEM   **HAM**

NIMROD   **CUSH**

JAPHETH

Parents: Have your child write the names of Noah's three sons, Nimrod and his father in the boxes of the family tree. Point out that Nimrod is the great grandson of Noah.

Originally published by the Worldwide Church of God
Produced in cooperation with Imperial Schools
Copyright© 1981. Reprint by *Continuing* Church of God • www.ccog.org

BIBLE MEMORY
God's Festivals

Passover
Days of Unleavened Bread
Pentecost
Feast of Trumpets
Day of Atonement
Feast of Tabernacles
Last Great Day

CROSSWORD PUZZLE

ACROSS
1. Did Nimrod and his followers obey God? __ __ .
2. Nimrod was a __ __ __ __ to the people.

DOWN
1. __ __ __ __ __ __ built a tower.
2. __ __ __ was one of Noah's three sons.

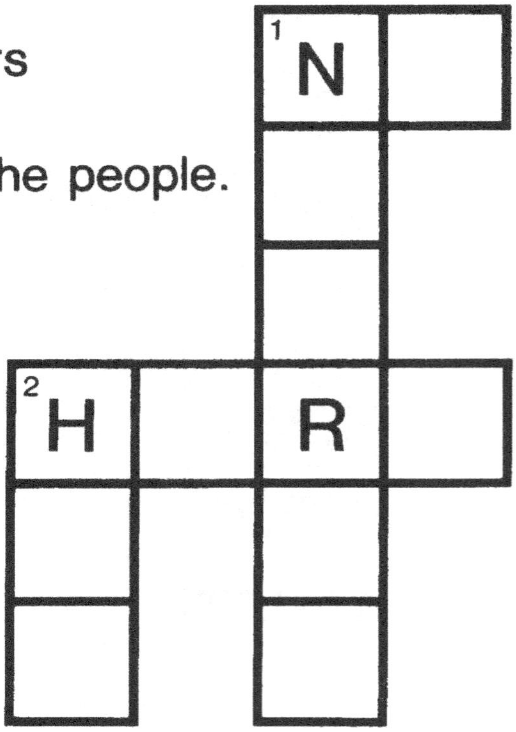

WORDS
Nimrod   Ham
Hero   No

Parents: To complete this crossword puzzle, read the questions or statements to your child. Also point out the answers under "WORDS." Also point out the already existing letters in the puzzle. Then have them write the correct letters in the boxes.

YOUTH BIBLE LESSONS

LEVEL 1

LESSON 6

Abraham–God's Obedient Servant

ABRAHAM—GOD'S OBEDIENT SERVANT

Many **generations** after Shem (a son of Noah), there was a man who became well-known for his obedience to God. This man's name was Abram, and his wife's name was Sarai. Later, we will learn that God changed their names to Abraham and Sarah.

When Abram was 75 years old, God spoke to him and told him to leave his home in Haran and to go to a land that He would show him. Abram did not question God as to why he was to go—he just obeyed. He packed up his belongings and took his wife, Sarai, and his **nephew** Lot with him. They settled in the land of Canaan.

Because of his obedience, Abram was blessed greatly by God. As the years went by, he became a very rich man. Many of his riches were in the form of sheep and cattle he owned. But there wasn't enough room in the area where they were living for both the herds of Abram and the herds of Lot. When their shepherds began to fight, Abram decided that he and Lot should go their separate ways.

Being a kind and **generous** man, Abram allowed Lot to choose whether he would stay where they were, or move on. Lot chose to move to the plains near the cities of Sodom and Gomorrah.

After Lot was gone, God spoke to Abram and told him to look in all directions from where he was. God said that He would give all that land to him and his **descendants.** He promised to bless Abram and make his descendants as many as the specks of dust on the earth.

It was hard for Abram and Sarai to understand how God was going to give them so many descendants. They were both getting older and as yet had no children. It took a great deal of faith for them to continue to believe God's promises.

When Abram was 99 years old, God spoke to him and changed his name to Abraham, which means "a father of many nations." At this time God also changed Sarai's name to Sarah. God told them that they would have a son and were to call him Isaac.

Some time later, the One who later became Jesus Christ **appeared** at Abraham's tent along with two angels. All three appeared as men. He told Abraham that Sarah would soon give birth to a son. He also told Abraham that the cities of Sodom and Gomorrah would be destroyed because of the **evil** the people were doing in these cities.

Abraham begged God not to destroy these cities if there were just a few **righteous** people living there. Remember, his nephew Lot and his family were living in the area. God finally told Abraham that he would not destroy the cities if only ten righteous people were there. But not even ten righteous people could be found!

God then sent the two angels to Sodom to tell Lot and his family to get out of the city because it was going to be **destroyed**. Lot and his family were **reluctant** to go at first, but finally went.

Lot and his family were warned not to look back at the city once they left. But Lot's wife could not **resist** taking one last look at her home. As punishment for her **disobedience**, God turned her into a pillar of salt. It is very important that we obey God and do what we are told!

When Abraham was 100 years old, Sarah had a son whom they named Isaac. God had kept His promise!

Up to this time, Abraham had done all that God asked him to do. However, God wanted to be sure that Abraham would obey Him by doing whatever He told him to do. So God decided to give Abraham a very difficult test.

One day, God told Abraham to take his son Isaac and offer him as a **burnt offering**. Abraham started to go to the mountains early the next morning. He was going to obey God. Abraham knew that if God did **require** him to **sacrifice** Isaac, God could also **resurrect** him. He also knew that God had promised to give him many children through Isaac.

After a three-day **journey**, Abraham finally reached the area where God told him to go. He then tied Isaac and placed him on the altar they had built. Abraham was about to **plunge** the knife into Isaac when he heard a voice ordering him to STOP! It was God speaking to him through an angel. Now God knew Abraham feared Him and would do anything He asked him to do! Isaac was a very happy young man! He and his father then saw a ram caught in a nearby bush and offered it for the offering.

Because Abraham was willing to withhold nothing from God, God again promised him that his descendants would be blessed. This is why the nations of Israel are so blessed today.

When Sarah was 127 years old she died. Later, Abraham married again. This time his wife's name was Keturah. Abraham continued to obey God the rest of his life. He was 175 years old when he died.

Parents: Explain all **boldface** words. You may wish to prompt further discussion by asking your child some of the following questions: Why did God tell Lot and his family not to look back? Why did Lot's wife turn into a pillar of salt? (Historians, like Josephus, reported seeing this pillar of salt over 1000 years later.)

Abraham and Lot go their separate ways.

Abraham learns that God will destroy Sodom and Gomorrah, and that Sarah will soon have a son.

Lot and his family leave Sodom.
Lot's wife disobeys by looking back
and becomes a pillar of salt.

As God promised, Abraham and Sarah did have a son whom they named Isaac.

Abraham left early in the morning to offer Isaac, as God told him to do.

When God knew that Abraham would obey Him, God provided a ram in the place of Isaac for the burnt offering.

Color the dotted rocks one color
and all other rocks another color,
to see the words that describe
Abraham's character.

Originally published by the Worldwide Church of God
Produced in cooperation with Imperial Schools
Copyright© 1981. Reprint by *Continuing* Church of God • www.ccog.org

BIBLE MEMORY
Books of the New Testament

1. Matthew
2. Mark
3. Luke
4. John
5. Acts
6. Romans
7. I Corinthians
8. II Corinthians
9. Galatians
10. Ephesians
11. Philippians
12. Colossians
13. I Thessalonians
14. II Thessalonians

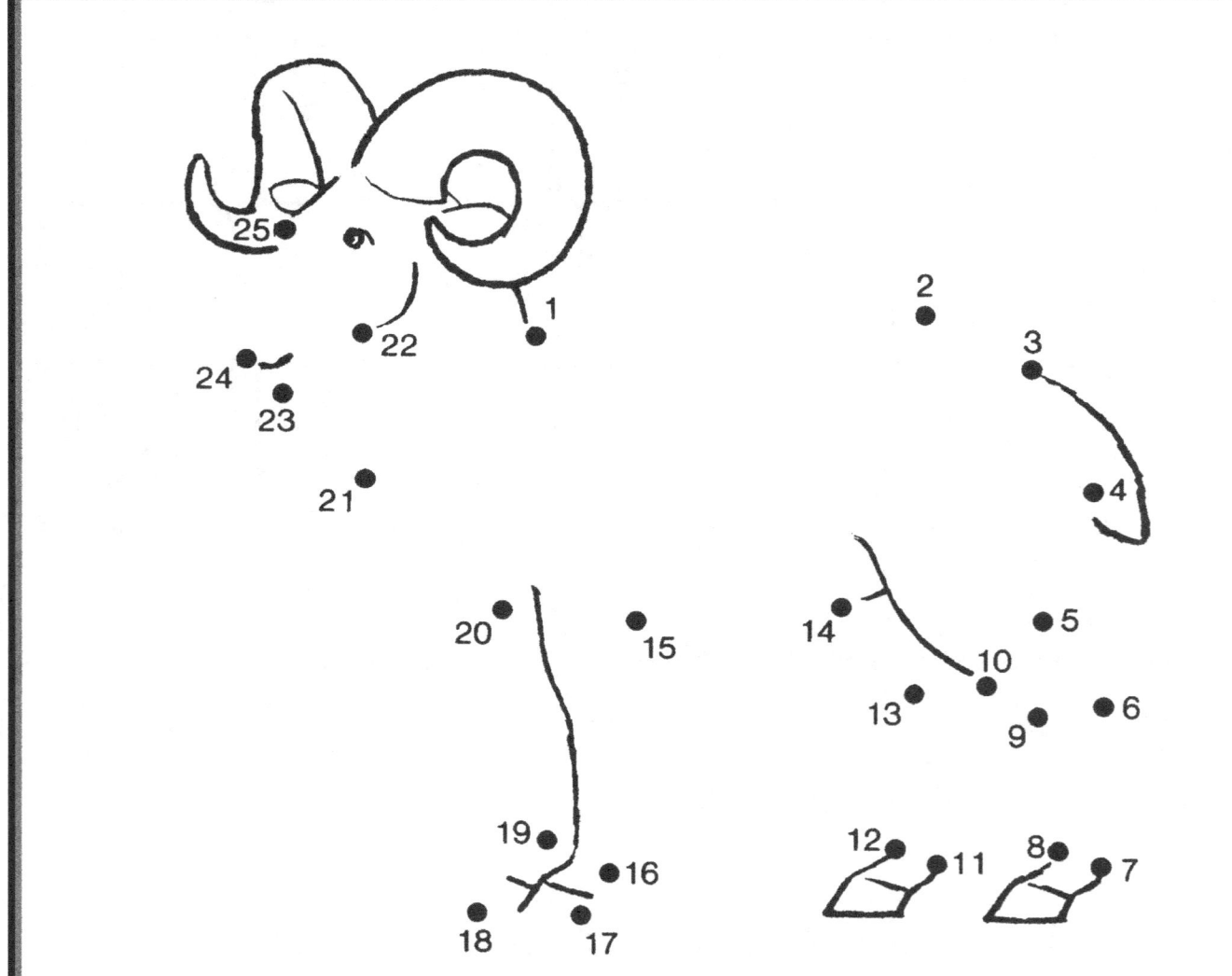

Connect the dots to find out what took Isaac's place as a burnt offering.

YOUTH BIBLE LESSONS

LEVEL

LESSON 7

Esau and Jacob

ESAU AND JACOB

Our last lesson ended with the death of Abraham. He was 175 years old when he died. But before his death, Abraham wanted to make sure that Isaac did not marry one of the women from Canaan. So Abraham told a **trusted** servant, "Go to where my father's family lives and bring back a wife for Isaac." God led the servant to Rebekah, the daughter of Abraham's nephew.

After Rebekah decided she would marry Isaac, the servant then returned home with Rebekah. Abraham was very happy when Isaac married her. Isaac was forty years old when he married Rebekah. For twenty years, Isaac and Rebekah could not have children. Isaac prayed to God about it and God answered his prayers. Rebekah would soon give birth to twins!

When the twins were born, they did not look alike. The first one born was red and hairy, but the second one born had smooth skin. Isaac and Rebekah named their firstborn son Esau and their second son Jacob.

As Esau and Jacob grew, they began to have different interests. Esau became a **rugged** hunter, spending much of his time out in the woods. Jacob stayed closer to home and kept the sheep.

Isaac loved Esau more than Jacob because he liked the

Parents: Explain the meaning of the **boldface** words. Read to your child the story of Abraham's servant finding a wife for Isaac (Genesis 24). Be sure to explain why Abraham did not want Isaac to marry a woman from Canaan. Also explain that it was a custom then for parents to choose whom their sons and daughters would marry. Tell your child that Esau and Jacob would become the fathers of two different nations.

venison which Esau brought home. But Rebekah loved Jacob more than Esau.

Because Esau was the firstborn son, he had the birthright. This meant that he would receive a larger part of his father's wealth when his father died.

One day Esau returned home from one of his hunting trips, dirty and **famished** from hunger. He could not resist an offer Jacob made to him. Jacob offered to sell Esau a bowl of **delicious**-smelling soup for his birthright.

Since Esau thought he would die without the food, he could not see what good his birthright would be. So Esau sold his birthright! Jacob should not have taken advantage of his brother to get something that did not belong to him.

When Isaac was old and blind and thought he might die soon, he called Esau to him. "Go out and get me some of the venison I love. I will then bless you."

But Rebekah overheard what Isaac told Esau. She wanted her favorite son, Jacob, to receive the blessing instead.

After Esau had gone out to hunt, Rebekah quickly planned how to trick Isaac into blessing Jacob while Esau was away. Jacob went along with the plan. Rebekah first sent him out to kill two young goats. She cooked the meat and then covered Jacob's hands and neck with the skins so he would feel hairy like Esau.

When everything was ready, Jacob entered his father's tent. "The meal you asked for is ready," he told his father. "I want you to bless me now." Isaac thought the voice he heard was Jacob's instead of Esau's. "Come closer to me so that I may feel you," Isaac said. When he felt Jacob's hairy arms, Isaac was **convinced** he was speaking to Esau.

When Isaac finished eating, he blessed Jacob. He said, "May God give you well-watered fields that will grow much food. Let people serve you and nations bow down to you. May a curse be on those who curse you and may a blessing be on those who bless you."

After the blessing, Jacob left his father and went outside. A few moments later, Esau came in with the meal of venison he had prepared. Esau was very angry when he learned what Jacob had done. The blessing could not be taken back and given to Esau, now that it had already been given to Jacob. Once again, Jacob had taken something that belonged to Esau.

Not long after this, Rebekah learned that Esau planned to kill Jacob as soon as Isaac died. Fearing for her favorite son's life, Rebekah asked Isaac to send Jacob far away to where her brother Laban lived, to find a wife. Since Isaac did not want his sons to marry women from Canaan, he agreed.

In our next lesson, we will pick up the story of Jacob's trip to his Uncle Laban's home. Some very important things happened during this trip.

Parents: Ask your child some of the following questions to prompt further discussion: Was it right for Jacob to ask Esau to sell his birthright for the soup? Why didn't Esau tell his father that he had sold his birthright? How did Jacob know when Isaac was going to bless Esau? Why was the blessing so important—what would it mean for Jacob's descendants? Why did Rebekah want Jacob to go to his Uncle Laban's home?

Esau liked to hunt in the woods.
Jacob stayed closer to home
and looked after the sheep.

Esau sells his birthright for Jacob's soup.

Jacob and his mother plan a way to steal Esau's blessing.

Isaac is tricked into blessing Jacob.

Rebekah says good-bye to her favorite son, not knowing when she will see him again.

TRUE OR FALSE

1. Abraham wanted Isaac to have a wife.   T   F

2. Esau was the firstborn twin.   T   F

3. Jacob was Isaac's favorite son.   T   F

4. Laban was Rebekah's father.   T   F

5. Esau was a hairy man.   T   F

6. Esau twice took something that was Jacob's.   T   F

7. Isaac married a woman from Canaan.   T   F

8. Jacob loved to hunt.   T   F

9. Isaac loved deer meat.   T   F

Parents: Read each sentence to your child and have him or her circle the "T" if it is true, or the "F" if it is false. You may need to explain the meaning of the word "false."

WHO RECEIVED THE BLESSING?

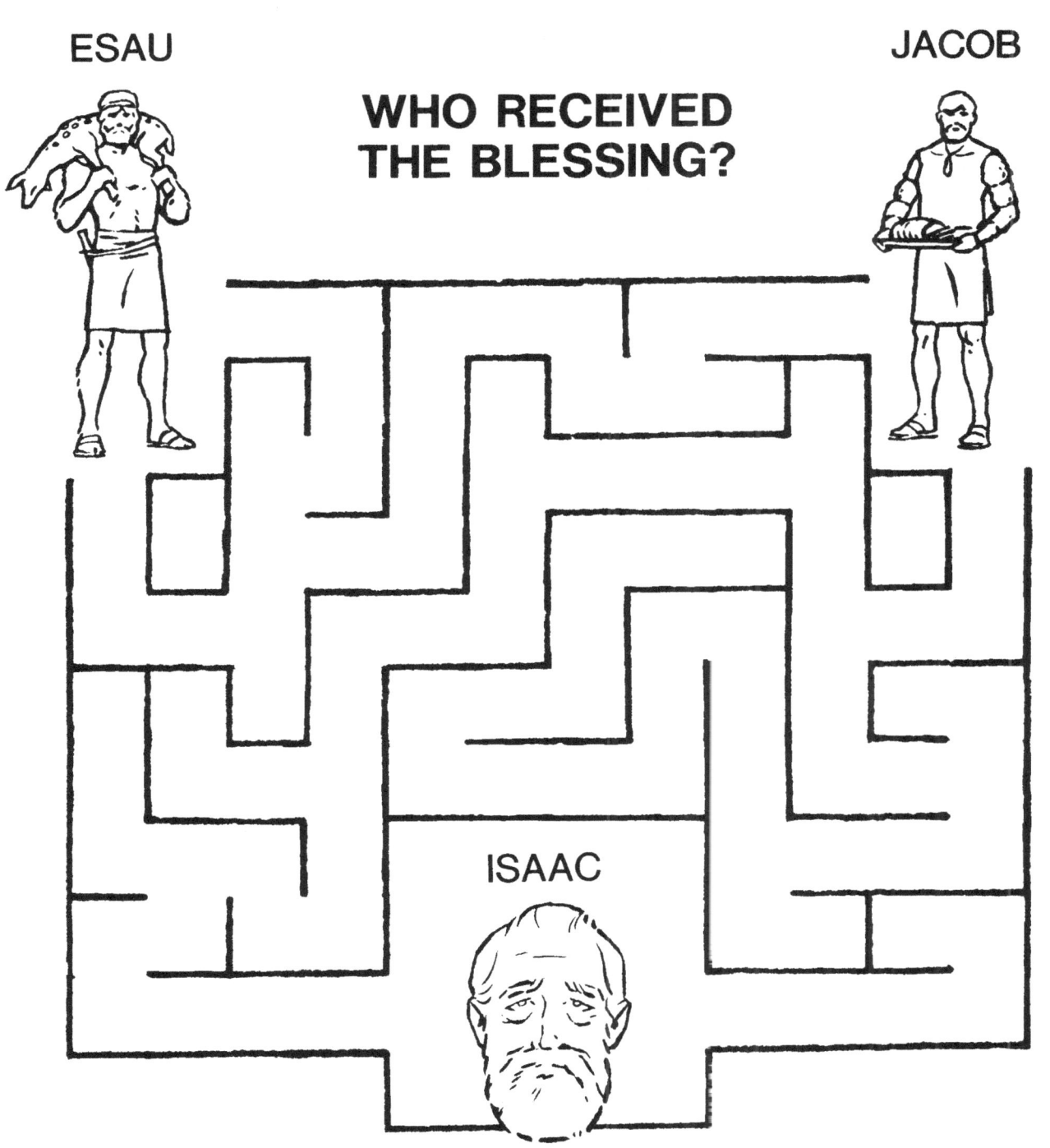

With a crayon, take the son who received the blessing through the maze to Isaac.

Originally published by the Worldwide Church of God
Produced in cooperation with Imperial Schools
Copyright© 1981. Reprint by *Continuing* Church of God • www.ccog.org

BIBLE MEMORY
Books of the
New Testament

1. I Timothy
2. II Timothy
3. Titus
4. Philemon
5. Hebrews
6. James
7. I Peter
8. II Peter
9. I John
10. II John
11. III John
12. Jude
13. Revelation

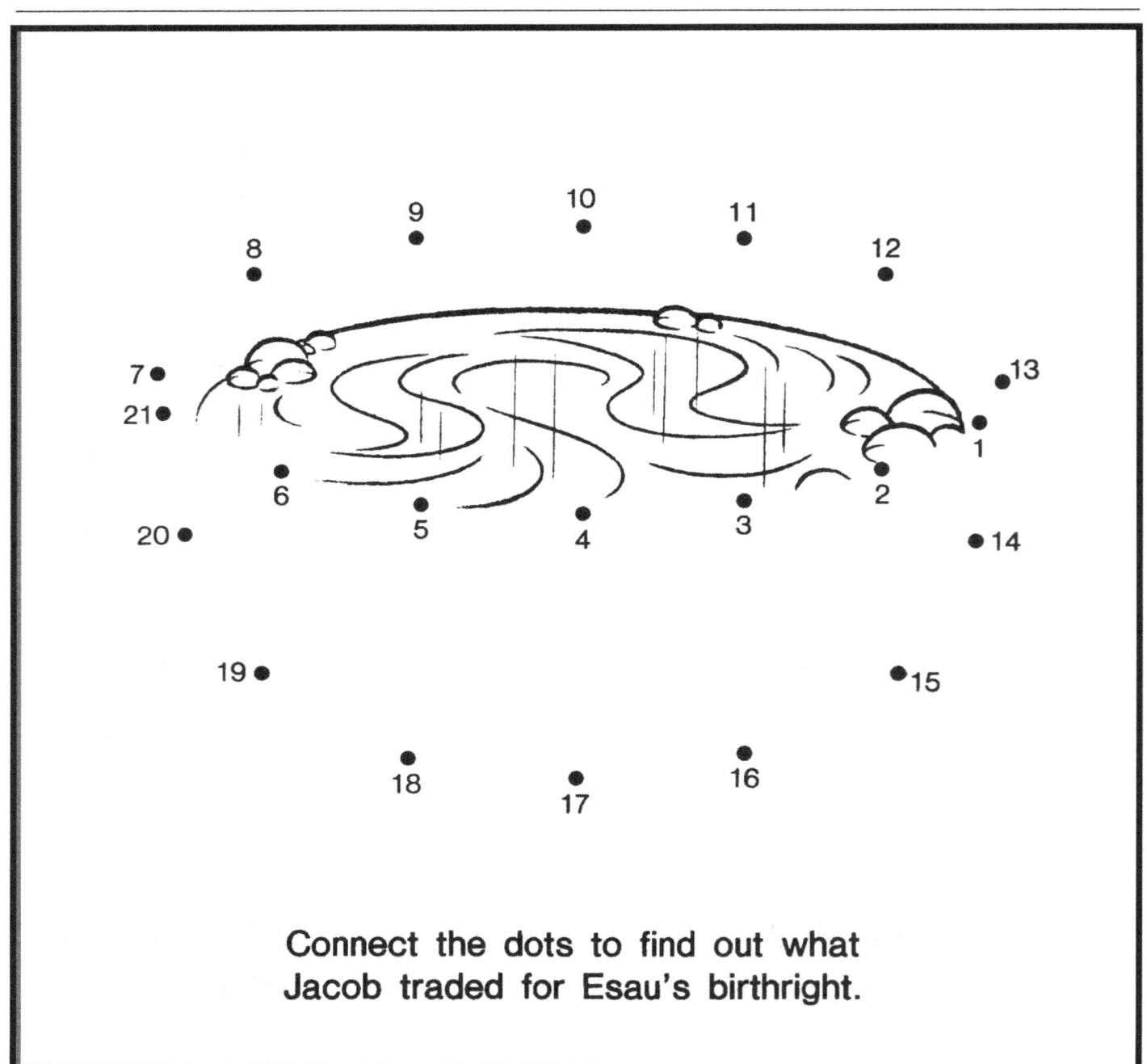

Connect the dots to find out what Jacob traded for Esau's birthright.

YOUTH BIBLE LESSONS

LEVEL

LESSON 8

Jacob and His Family

JACOB AND HIS FAMILY

After Jacob left for his Uncle Laban's home, he stopped for the night on a rock-covered mountain slope. There he slept on the ground with his head resting on a large stone.

While Jacob slept, he dreamed of a ladder that reached from earth to heaven. There were many angels walking up and down the ladder. Standing above the ladder was God.

God spoke to Jacob and said, "The land on which you lie I will give to you and your **descendants**. They will spread out to many parts of the earth." God also promised to bless and **protect** him wherever he went.

Then Jacob awakened. He knew that God had been there and realized this was a special place. So he set up the large stone his head had been resting on as a **pillar** to mark the place. He poured oil on it and named the place Bethel, which means "House of God." Jacob then continued his journey to his Uncle Laban's home.

JACOB MEETS RACHEL

After traveling for many days, Jacob saw shepherds in the distance bringing their flocks to a well. As he came near the well, Jacob asked them where they were from. "We are from Haran," they said.

"Do you know my Uncle Laban?" Jacob asked.

Parents: Explain the meaning of the **boldface** words. Also, explain that the way God speaks to us today is through His written Word, the Bible.

"We know him, and he is doing well," the shepherds answered.

Just then, Laban's daughter Rachel arrived at the well to water her father's sheep. As Jacob and Rachel talked, they were excited to learn that they were cousins. Rachel hurried home to tell her father about meeting Jacob.

Laban was happy to see Jacob, and invited him to stay with them. During the next month, Jacob worked around the house and in the fields. When Laban asked him what **wages** he would like for his work, Jacob said, "I will work seven years for you if at the end of that time you will give me Rachel for my wife." Laban agreed.

After the seven years Jacob was married. After the wedding he was surprised to discover that Laban had tricked him into marrying Leah instead of Rachel! Laban explained to Jacob that it was the **custom** in their land for the older daughter to marry before the younger. Laban then promised to give him Rachel at the end of the week if he would work for him seven more years! Jacob agreed.

Jacob loved Rachel more than Leah. But Rachel was unable to have children. During the next five years, Leah had four sons. She named them Reuben, Simeon, Levi and Judah.

Rachel was very sad because of this, so she had her maid Bilhah have children for her. Bilhah gave birth to two sons who were named Dan and Naphtali. Then, Leah decided that her maid, Zilpah, should also have children for her. Zilpah had two sons whom Leah named Gad and Asher. Later, Leah herself had two more sons, Issachar and Zebulun, and a daughter she named Dinah.

After this, God healed Rachel so that she was able to have children. In time, she gave birth to a son whom she named

---

Parents: Remind your child that Jacob had tricked Esau years earlier, and was now tricked himself. Also explain that Jacob did not see the bride's face until after the wedding.

Joseph. This made Rachel very happy.

JACOB RETURNS TO CANAAN

At the end of the second seven years, Jacob decided to work for Laban six more years. Altogether he worked a total of twenty years for Laban.

During this time, Jacob's family had grown very large. He had also become very wealthy. Jacob now wanted to leave Laban and return to the land of Canaan where his father Isaac lived. But Laban did not want Jacob to leave. So Jacob and his family left at a time when Laban was away.

Unknown to Jacob, Rachel stole some of her father's images and took them with her. When Laban returned home, he was angry to learn that Jacob and his family had gone. Laban then went after them. After seven days, he caught up with Jacob and his family. Laban searched their tents, but could not find the images. He returned home and Jacob continued on his way.

Nearing the land of Canaan, Jacob learned that his brother Esau and a group of his men were on their way to meet him. Jacob was worried about how Esau, whom he had not seen for twenty years, would treat him when they met. After asking God for protection, Jacob put his men and servants in the front of the caravan and kept his wives and children behind.

Before they met, both groups camped for the night. While his caravan was setting up camp, Jacob stayed a short distance behind to pray.

Suddenly, somebody grabbed him and a wrestling match began. Jacob soon realized that his opponent wasn't an ordinary man. He was the Eternal, the One who later became Jesus Christ!

Parents: Ask your child why Jacob was worried about meeting Esau.

The two wrestled all night, but Jacob would not let go until God had blessed him. So God blessed Jacob and changed his name to Israel.

The next morning, as Esau came near, Jacob stepped forward and bowed himself seven times. This was the custom when one wanted to show respect.

Esau came closer and closer, and then rushed toward Jacob and hugged him! The two brothers were happy to be together again. God had answered Jacob's prayer.

After Esau met Jacob's family, he and Jacob went their separate ways. Jacob continued his journey to where Isaac lived. On the way, Rachel gave birth to Jacob's twelfth son, Benjamin. Rachel died after giving birth to Benjamin.

Jacob finally reached the land of Canaan and lived there for many years. His father Isaac died at the age of 180. As Jacob's sons grew older, they helped to tend the sheep. Jacob loved all of his sons, but he had a special love for his son Joseph.

We will learn more about Joseph in the next lesson, and about the many miracles that God worked in his life.

Parents: Explain that the descendants of Jacob's sons have become certain nations today. Also explain that "Israel" means champion or overcomer.

Jacob dreams of a ladder reaching from earth to heaven.

Jacob agrees to work for Laban seven years in order to marry Rachel.

Jacob is shocked when he discovers Laban has tricked him into marrying his oldest daughter Leah!

Jacob wrestles all night with the One who later became Jesus Christ.

Jacob and his brother Esau are happy to see each other.

Write a number 1 in the circles beside the pictures of things Jacob could have seen in his time. Write a number 2 in the circles beside the pictures of things Jacob could not have seen.

BIBLE MEMORY
Ten Commandments

You shall have no other gods before God.
You shall not make any graven image of God.
You shall not take His name in vain.
Remember the Sabbath day and keep it holy.
You shall honor your father and mother.
You shall not murder.
You shall not commit adultery.
You shall not steal.
You shall not lie.
You shall not covet what is your neighbor's.

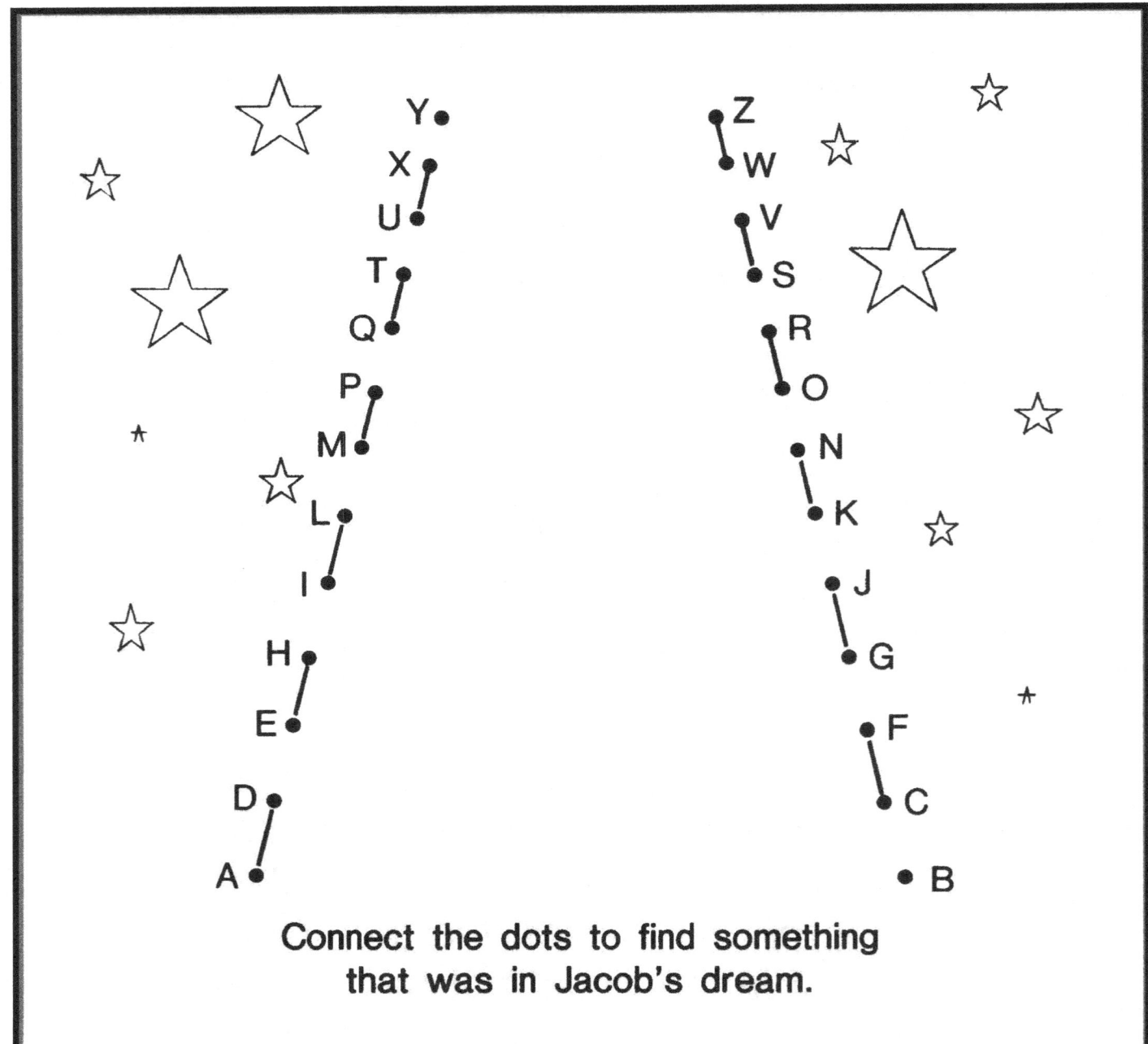

Connect the dots to find something that was in Jacob's dream.

YOUTH BIBLE LESSONS

LEVEL

LESSON 9

Joseph's Adventures in Egypt

JOSEPH'S ADVENTURES IN EGYPT

Joseph was the firstborn son of Rachel, Jacob's favorite wife. Jacob loved Joseph more than his other sons, and gave him a beautiful coat of many colors.

Joseph's brothers became very jealous when they saw that their father loved him more than he loved them. This jealousy grew into hatred. They hated Joseph even more when he told them about his dreams of some day ruling over them.

One day, when Joseph was about seventeen, his brothers went a long distance from home to feed their father's flocks. When they had been gone for several days, Jacob called Joseph and said, "Go find your brothers and see how they're doing."

After much searching, Joseph finally found his brothers. When they saw him coming, they said to one another, "Here comes that dreamer. Let's kill him and tell our father that a wild animal killed and ate him." But Reuben, the oldest brother, said, "No, let's not kill him. Let's just drop him into a nearby **well**."

As Joseph came near, his brothers suddenly grabbed him. They ripped off his coat of many colors and dropped him into an empty well. Then they sat down to eat.

While eating, they noticed a **caravan** of traders passing nearby on its way to Egypt. "Let's sell Joseph to these traders and make a profit," one of his brothers suggested. They agreed

---

Parents: Explain the meaning of the **boldface** words. Discuss with your child the dreams that Joseph had as a teenager. They are found in Genesis 37.

and sold him for a small sum of money. Not wanting their father to know the truth, they took Joseph's coat and smeared it with the blood of a goat they had killed.

When Joseph's brothers returned home, they showed the coat to their father and said, "We found this coat. Is it your son's coat or not?"

Seeing the blood-stained coat, Jacob thought that Joseph had been killed by a wild animal. He was very, very sad.

JOSEPH A SLAVE IN EGYPT

When the traders reached Egypt they sold Joseph to Potiphar, who was an **officer** of Pharaoh, king of Egypt. Joseph became a servant in Potiphar's house. It wasn't long before Potiphar saw that Joseph did all his jobs very well. So he put Joseph in charge of all his servants. God was blessing Joseph in all that he did because he kept His commandments.

Joseph continued to serve his master well until Potiphar's wife **falsely accused** him of trying to harm her. When Potiphar heard this, he became angry and had Joseph put in prison. God was allowing these events for a purpose, as we will soon see.

Joseph continued to set a fine example in his work and his attitude. The keeper of the prison noticed this and decided to put Joseph in charge of all the prisoners.

Meanwhile, Pharaoh's **butler** and **baker** were put in the prison. One night, each of them had a dream. When they awoke the next morning, they were both very sad. Joseph noticed this and asked, "Why are you so sad?"

"We have each dreamed a dream," they said. "But there is no one to tell us what they mean."

Then Joseph said, "Do not **interpretations** belong to God? Tell me your dreams."

"I dreamed of a vine with three branches that had many

clusters of grapes," the butler said. "I took the grapes and squeezed the juice from them into Pharaoh's cup."

God instantly put the meaning of the dream in Joseph's mind. "In three days you will return to your job in Pharaoh's court," Joseph told the butler. "When this happens, please remember me. I was put in prison without having done anything wrong."

The baker then told Joseph his dream. "I dreamed of three baskets on top of my head," he said. "The top basket was filled with food for the king. Then birds came and ate the food from the basket."

"Your dream means that in three days you will be hanged," Joseph told the frightened baker.

In three days, both dreams came to pass — just as Joseph had said. The butler returned to work for Pharaoh and the baker was hanged. The butler was happy to be free. But he forgot all about Joseph.

JOSEPH BECOMES RULER OF EGYPT UNDER PHARAOH

Two years later, while Joseph was still in prison, Pharaoh had two dreams that worried him. None of his wise men could understand the meaning of the dreams. Then the butler remembered how Joseph had given him the meaning of his dream, and told Pharaoh about him.

"Have him brought before me at once!" ordered Pharaoh. Joseph was soon standing before the king of Egypt. With God's help, he told Pharaoh the meaning of his dreams.

"God has shown Pharaoh what He is about to do," said Joseph. "There will be seven years of good crops followed by seven years of terrible **famine**. You would be wise to put someone in charge of storing grain during the good years to save for the years of famine."

After hearing Joseph's wise advice, Pharaoh decided to make him ruler, or governor, of all Egypt under him. He put Joseph in charge of storing grain for the coming famine. God was greatly blessing Joseph because of his continued obedience.

After the seven good years, the famine began as Joseph foretold. When people ran out of food, they went to Joseph who sold them the amount of grain they needed.

The famine was very great in Canaan too. Hearing that the Egyptians were selling grain, Jacob sent ten of his sons there to buy some. He kept his youngest son Benjamin at home for fear of losing him as he had lost Joseph several years earlier.

Joseph **recognized** his brothers when they came to buy the grain, but they did not recognize him. He wanted to welcome them, but decided to be **harsh** with them for a while to teach them a lesson.

"You are spies!" he accused his brothers. "We are not," they replied. But Joseph had them put in prison anyway. Three days later, he released them all, except for Simeon.

Joseph said to his frightened brothers, "I shall keep your brother Simeon here in prison. The rest of you may return home. When you bring your younger brother Benjamin, I'll know you are telling the truth and will release Simeon. Don't come back to Egypt for more grain unless you bring Benjamin with you!" The brothers returned home and told their father all that happened. But Jacob refused to let Benjamin go to Egypt.

JOSEPH REVEALS HIS IDENTITY

The famine continued to worsen, and once again Jacob's food supply was low. He had no choice but to let Benjamin go to

---

Parents: Explain what Pharaoh's dreams were, and how Joseph was able to interpret their meaning.

Egypt. So Joseph's brothers quickly returned to Egypt for more food.

Joseph invited them to eat lunch with him, but did not tell them who he was. The next day they received their grain and began the long trip home.

Suddenly, they saw men on horses riding toward them! The leader was Joseph's chief servant. "Why have you stolen the governor's favorite silver cup?" he demanded.

"We are not thieves," they explained. But after a search was made, the cup was found in Benjamin's sack of grain. Earlier, Joseph had the silver cup placed in Benjamin's sack. Now the brothers would have to go back to Egypt and appear before Joseph to explain.

Looking at his fearful brothers, Joseph pointed at Benjamin and said, "You will stay here and be my servant. The rest of you may return home."

"But our father will die of sorrow if Benjamin does not return with us," pleaded Judah, the brother responsible for Benjamin.

Joseph was unable to hold back his true **identity** from his brothers any longer. With tears streaming down his face, he cried out, "I am Joseph your brother, whom you sold!" His brothers were surprised and frightened!

"Don't be fearful," said Joseph. "God has caused events to work out so that I would be here to help prepare for the famine. I want you to return to Canaan and bring your father, your families and all your **possessions** to Egypt."

When the brothers returned home, they told their father about the unusual turn of events. Jacob was shocked, but very happy to hear that Joseph was still alive. When he arrived in Egypt, Jacob was happy to see the son whom he thought was

---

Parents: Explain why Joseph treated his brothers so harshly. Also, explain why Jacob crossed his arms when he blessed Manasseh and Ephraim, and explain who their modern-day descendants are.

dead. He and his family were allowed by Pharaoh to live in the part of Egypt called Goshen.

Just before he died, Jacob adopted Joseph's two sons, Manasseh and Ephraim, as his own. Jacob then crossed his arms and blessed his two grandchildren, asking God to give the greater blessing to Ephraim, the younger brother. Jacob then blessed his own sons, after which he died at the age of 147. His body was taken to the land of Canaan where he was buried.

Joseph and all his brothers and their families continued to live in the land of Egypt. There they grew great in number. Joseph continued to live a full and eventful life with God's blessing until his death at the age of 110.

WORD SEARCH In the puzzle below, find the six words listed to the right and draw a circle around them. The letters may go up, down, across or backwards. The first word is done for you.

```
D J A L M N M O
P O T I P H A R
B B C K A R E P
O A W E L L R Q
C M R G C H D T
A O O Y V J S V
J M H P E S O J
Z X Y T T N P W
```

DREAM ✓
EGYPT
JACOB
JOSEPH
POTIPHAR
WELL

Joseph was dropped into an empty well by his brothers.

Joseph is thrown in prison.

Benjamin finds Joseph's favorite silver cup in his sack of grain!

Parents: Explain why Joseph had his silver cup placed in Benjamin's sack of grain.

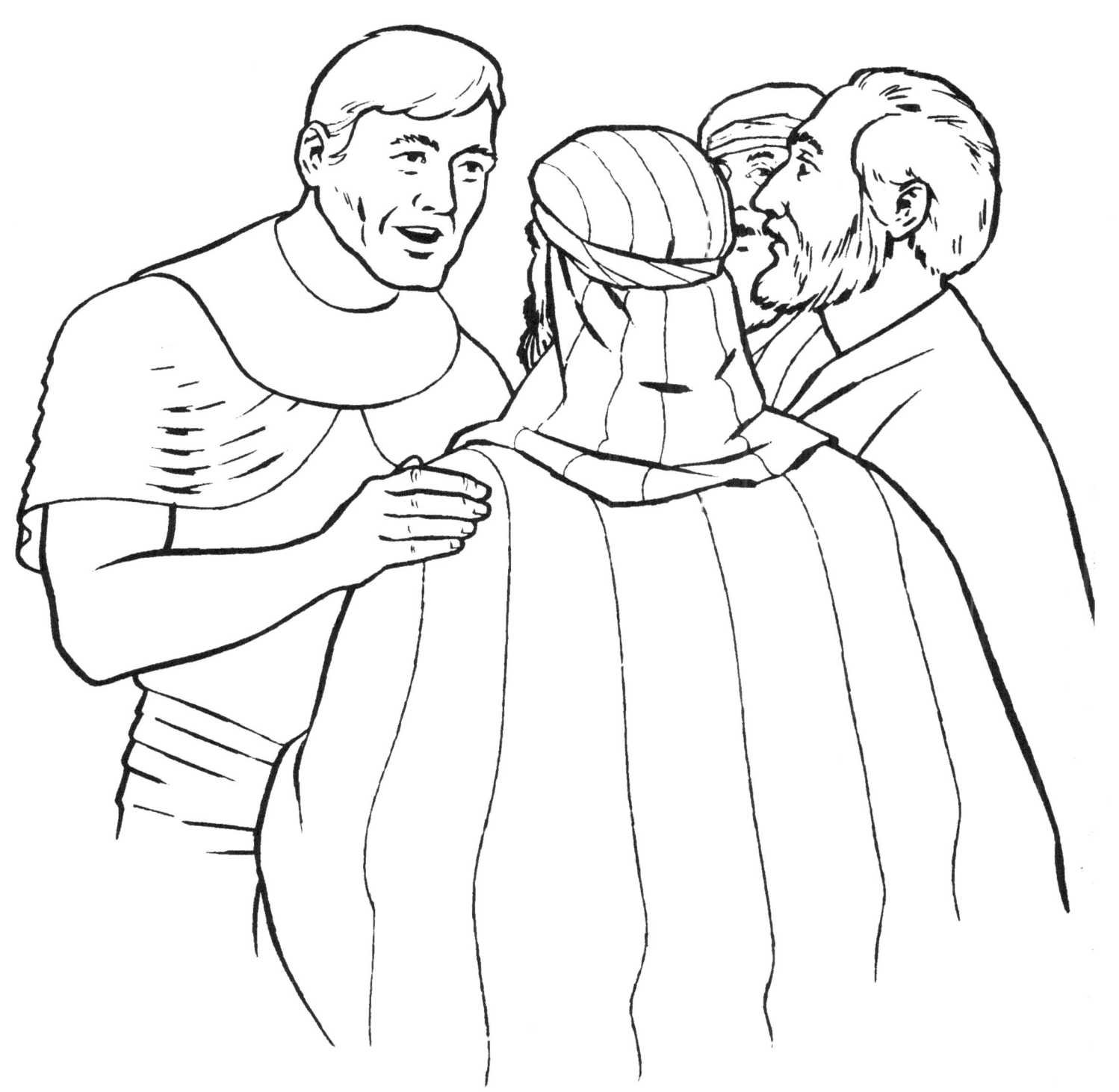

Joseph tells his brothers who he is!

BIBLE MEMORY Ephesians 6:1-3

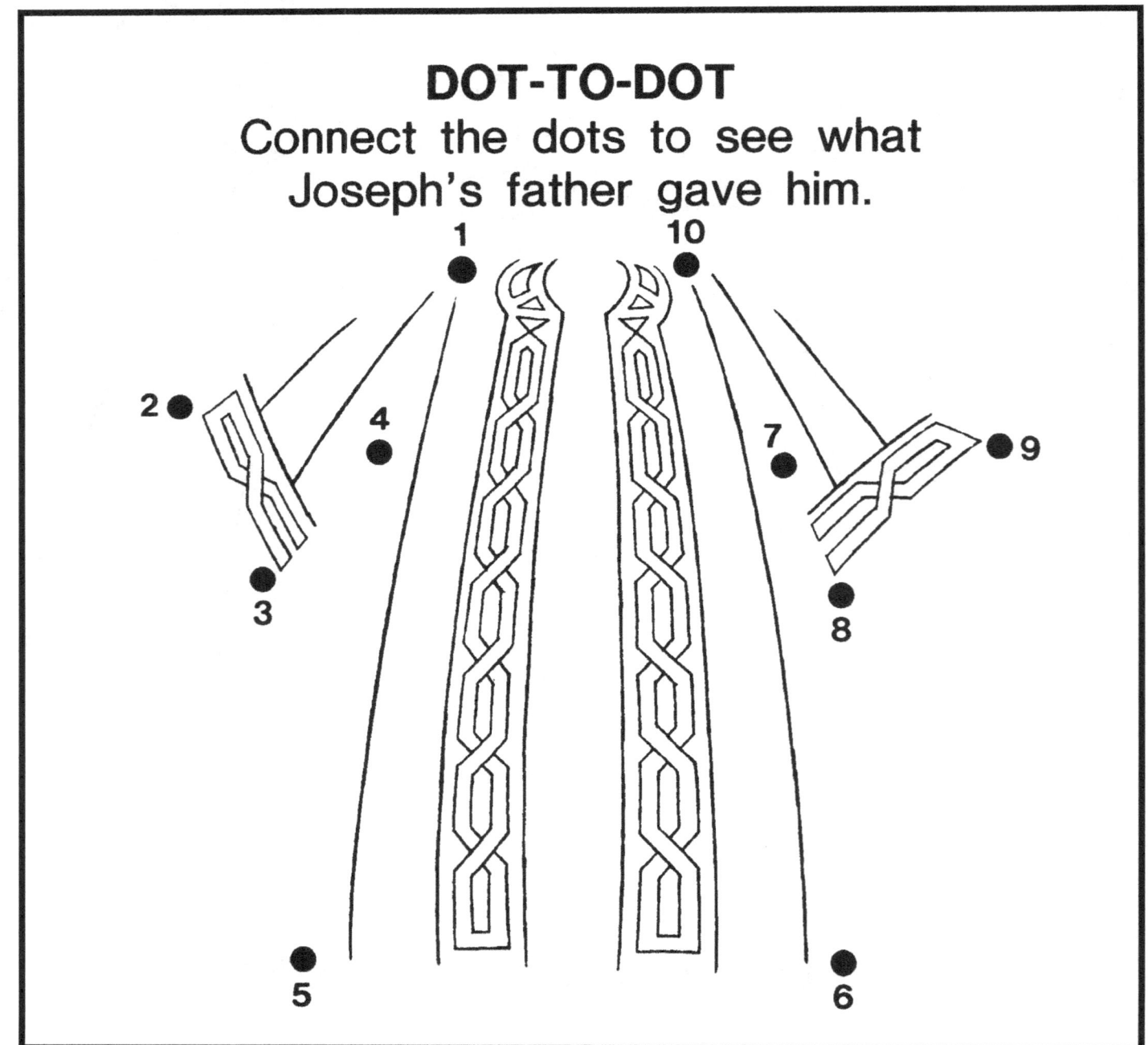

DOT-TO-DOT
Connect the dots to see what Joseph's father gave him.

YOUTH BIBLE LESSONS

LEVEL

LESSON 10

God Calls Moses

GOD CALLS MOSES

After the death of Joseph and his brothers, their families continued to live in the land of Egypt. There they grew great in number and later became known as **Israelites**.

After many years, a new Pharaoh became king of Egypt. He was very mean to the Israelites. He made them **slaves** under harsh **taskmasters**. The Israelites were made to work very hard.

Pharaoh thought this would stop them from having more children. But the harder the Israelites worked, the more children they had.

Then Pharaoh told the **midwives** to kill all the newborn Israelite boys. But the midwives did not obey Pharaoh. They obeyed God and did not kill the baby boys. God blessed them for obeying Him and gave them houses to live in.

One day, a baby boy was born to one of the Israelite women. He was a very handsome baby. His mother hid him for three months. She did not want him to be killed by Pharaoh's soldiers.

When she could no longer hide her son, she put him in a small reed basket. Carefully she smeared it with **pitch**. Then she set the basket among the bulrushes of the Nile River, and sent her daughter along to see what would happen.

Soon the young girl saw Pharaoh's daughter find the basket floating among the bulrushes. When Pharaoh's daughter opened the basket, she saw the baby boy inside. Happily she took him from the basket. The baby's sister excitedly ran to Pharaoh's daughter. "Will you need someone to nurse the child?" she asked. "Yes, go and find an Israelite to nurse the child!" Pharaoh's daughter ordered. The young girl quickly ran to tell her mother.

Because the child's mother trusted God, He allowed her to care for her own son. But before long, Pharaoh's daughter returned and took him back to be a prince in Pharaoh's court. She named him Moses.

As Moses grew into a man, he thought about the Israelites **suffering** as slaves. One day he went to see them. On the way, Moses saw an Egyptian hitting one of the Israelite slaves. Moses was angered. After looking to see if others were watching, he killed the Egyptian.

Moses knew he should not have killed the Egyptian and hoped that no one saw him. But later, Moses learned that someone did see him.

Pharaoh soon heard that Moses had killed an Egyptian. Knowing his life was in danger, Moses quickly fled to the land of Midian. While in the land of Midian, Moses stayed with a man named Reuel (also called Jethro). Moses later married Jethro's daughter, Zipporah.

Many more years passed. The Israelites, who were very sad, were still slaves in Egypt. They worked very hard to make bricks for Pharaoh's buildings. God saw how the Egyptians treated the Israelites and decided to help them. He called Moses to lead them out of slavery.

Moses was tending his father-in-law's sheep near Mount Sinai. As he was herding the flocks, God appeared to Moses in a burning bush. Moses went closer to see the bush as it burned. He was surprised when he saw that the bush was not burning

---

Parents: Explain the meaning of the **boldface** words. Discuss with your child why it was wrong for Moses to kill the Egyptian. Also, explain why he was given the name, Moses.

up. God then spoke to Moses, "Take off your shoes!" God's voice boomed. "You are standing on holy ground." God then told Moses to go and tell Pharaoh to free the Israelites.

"How will they know that You have sent me?" Moses asked. "Cast down your shepherd's rod!" God commanded Moses. When Moses threw his rod to the ground, it became a snake. When he grabbed it by the tail, it became a shepherd's rod again.

God also performed another **miracle** by causing Moses' hand to become **leprous** and be healed again. Moses could use these miracles to show that God had called him to go before the Pharaoh.

But Moses was afraid to face the king of Egypt. He explained to God that he could not speak well. So God agreed to let Moses' brother, Aaron, go with him and talk to Pharaoh.

God told Moses that Pharaoh would not want to free the Israelites. God knew He would have to perform great miracles before Pharaoh would let them go.

Moses and Aaron then went to see Pharaoh. They asked Pharaoh to free the Israelites. This made the king angry. He made the Israelites work harder than before. Now they had to make more bricks and gather the straw, also.

Later, Moses and Aaron went to see Pharaoh again. This time God did miracles before Pharaoh by turning the shepherd's rod into a snake. But Pharaoh would not let the Israelites go.

In our next lesson, we will learn about the **plagues** God sent upon Pharaoh and the Egyptians.

Parents: Explain how the people of Israel came to be in the land of Egypt. Also explain what made the ground holy where Moses was standing. Discuss with your child the miracles that God performed through Moses before Pharaoh.

Moses is placed into a small basket by his mother.

Pharaoh's daughter finds Moses floating among the bulrushes.

Moses flees to the land of Midian.

God speaks to Moses from the burning bush.

Moses and Aaron ask Pharaoh to let the Israelites leave Egypt.

WHICH WOMAN IS MOSES' MOTHER?

Follow the paths to see which one leads to Moses.

Connect the dots to see what Moses saw when God called him.

BIBLE MEMORY   Matthew 5:3-8

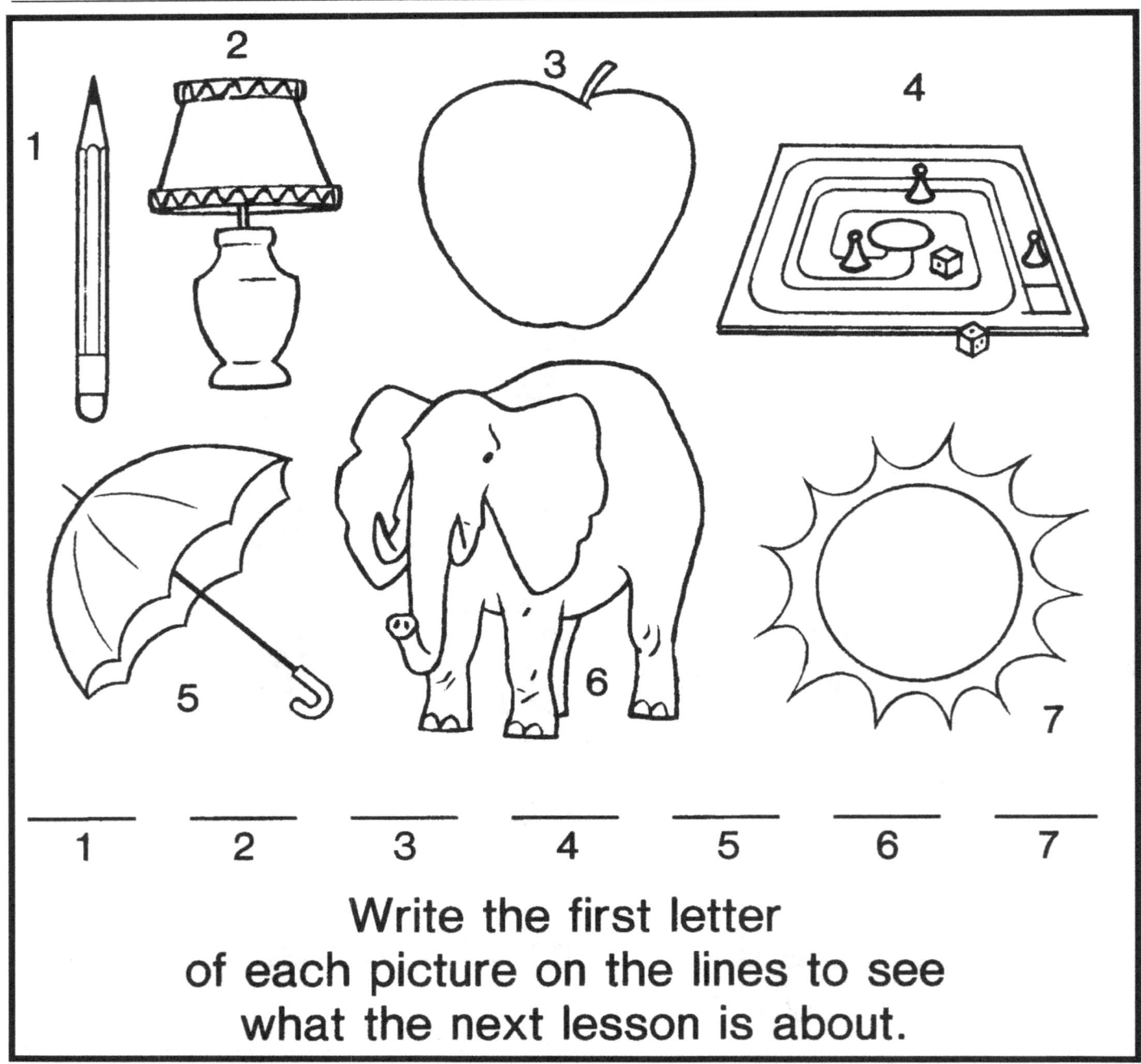

YOUTH BIBLE LESSONS

LEVEL 1

LESSON 11

The Plagues on Egypt

THE PLAGUES ON EGYPT

God warned Moses that Pharaoh would not free the Israelites from slavery. God knew that Pharaoh would have to see great miracles before he would let them go.

For the second time Moses and Aaron arrived at Pharaoh's palace. Pharaoh and his **magicians** were there. This time Pharaoh wanted to see **proof** of God's power, so Aaron threw his rod to the floor and it became a large, wiggling snake. Pharaoh's magicians did the same with their rods and they became snakes.

However, everyone was surprised when Aaron's snake ate up the magician's snakes. Still, Pharaoh would not let the Israelites go.

God then told Moses and Aaron to see Pharaoh the next morning. They were to meet Pharaoh at the river and ask him to free the Israelites.

Moses and Aaron got up early the next morning and went to the river. There they found Pharaoh as he was about to take a bath. "God has sent us to ask you to let the Israelites go," Moses and Aaron told Pharaoh. "If not, your waters will be turned to blood."

"I will not let your people go!" Pharaoh scoffed. "Let us see if you can turn the waters to blood."

Aaron then raised his rod high over his head and brought

Parents: Explain the meaning of the **boldface** words.

it quickly down into the water. Pharaoh watched with surprise as the water began to turn red. In a few moments, the river and all the ponds and streams of Egypt became blood.

After seven days, God told Moses and Aaron to again ask Pharaoh to let the Israelites go. But Pharaoh would not let them go.

God then told Moses and Aaron to hold the rod out over the rivers, streams and ponds of Egypt. When they did, **millions** of frogs came up out of the waters. They went all over the land. They got in people's rooms, clothes and food. Frogs were everywhere!

Pharaoh quickly called for Moses and Aaron to take away the frogs. "Ask your God to take away these frogs and I will let your people go," Pharaoh told Moses.

Moses and Aaron were **encouraged**, thinking they would soon be leaving Egypt. Moses prayed to God and the frogs stopped coming from the waters. The plague was now over, but there were still many dead frogs to clean up. Pharaoh now decided there was no reason to let the Israelites go. So God sent a third plague upon the Egyptians.

Aaron took his rod and hit the ground and the dust became lice. The lice were everywhere, on the people and on the animals. Yet the pain and **itching** from the lice was not enough to make Pharaoh change his mind. He would not free the Israelites.

Again, God sent a fourth plague on the Egyptians. "Since you will not let the people go," Moses and Aaron said to Pharaoh, "God will send biting flies into your land, but the flies will not hurt the Israelites in Goshen."

Then swarms of flies came, biting and stinging the Egyptians and their animals. Again Pharaoh called for Moses and Aaron and

---

Parents: Explain to your child why Pharaoh did not want to free the Israelites. Also, explain what happened on the first Passover and why we celebrate the Night to Be Much Observed today.

promised to let the people go if God would stop the plague. When the plague ended, Pharaoh again changed his mind.

Now God sent a fifth plague upon the animals of the Egyptians. The next day, the Egyptian's cattle, horses, camels, sheep and other animals began to die from a **disease**. However, the plague did not **harm** the Israelites' animals. Pharaoh lost many of his cattle, but he would not free the Israelites.

God next told Moses to take handfuls of **ashes** from a **furnace** and throw them into the air in front of Pharaoh. Whenever these ashes touched the Egyptians' skin, they became **boils**. They were very painful. The Egyptians could not walk because of the boils. Even the magicians could not stand before Moses. Still Pharaoh would not listen to Moses and free the Israelites. Pharaoh was very **stubborn**.

Moses warned Pharaoh and the Egyptians that anyone who stayed in the fields with their cattle the next day would be killed. God would now send large **hailstones** and lightning.

A few of Pharaoh's servants obeyed Moses and brought their cattle and animals inside. However, many Egyptians and their animals were caught in the plague and died. But the Israelites did not have the storm in the land of Goshen.

Once again Pharaoh called for Moses and Aaron. Pharaoh told them that he would not let the people go.

The eighth plague was locusts. They swarmed through the land eating plants, flowers and fruit trees. They also ate what was left of the Egyptians' **crops**. This time Pharaoh said he had sinned and would now let the people go free. So God caused a strong wind to blow the locusts into the Red Sea. When they were gone, Pharaoh changed his mind again.

Because Pharaoh would not keep his word, God caused a thick darkness to come over the land of Egypt. It was so dark that the Egyptians could not see to walk. They could not see each other. The thick darkness lasted for three days. But this did not make Pharaoh let the people go.

God told Moses there would be only one more plague and then Pharaoh would free the Israelites. As you learned in the Spring Feast Lesson, this 10th and final plague was what happened on the first Passover. The last plague was the death of all the firstborn of the Egyptians.

When Pharaoh saw his firstborn son dead, he called for Moses and Aaron and told them to leave the land of Egypt. The Israelites did leave and took all their families and animals with them. The night they left was called the Night to Be Much Observed, which we keep today.

Though some of the world's educated do not wish to believe it, there is historical evidence of many of the plagues that God smote Egypt with.

Aaron strikes the water with his rod
and the water becomes blood.

God causes frogs to come from the rivers, streams and ponds of Egypt.

God turns the dust into lice as Aaron's rod hits the ground.

Biting and stinging flies swarm over the land of Egypt.

The fifth plague kills many of the Egyptians' animals.

Moses throws the ashes into the air, causing painful boils on the Egyptians.

The hailstones and lightning struck those who did not listen to Moses' warning.

The locusts quickly eat all that is left of the crops.

God brings darkness over the land of Egypt.

Originally published by the Worldwide Church of God
Produced in cooperation with Imperial Schools
Copyright© 1981. Reprint by *Continuing* Church of God • www.ccog.org

BIBLE MEMORY   Matthew 5:9-12

Connect the dots to see what God told Moses and Aaron to use to turn the waters into blood.

YOUTH BIBLE LESSONS

LEVEL

SPECIAL FEAST LESSON

The Fall Feasts

FALL FESTIVAL EDITION

Feast of Trumpets

Day of Atonement

Feast of Tabernacles

Packing our suitcases

Loading the car

Did you come to the Feast by plane?

Did you come to the Feast by ship?

Did you come to the Feast by bus?

Did you come to the Feast by train?

Did you come to the Feast by car?

YOUTH BIBLE LESSONS

LEVEL

SPECIAL FEAST LESSON

The Spring Feasts

SPRING FESTIVAL EDITION

THE SPRING FEASTS

God wants everyone who has ever lived to become members of His Family. This is His wonderful purpose for creating human beings.

God also has a plan which shows how we may come into His Family. The feast days we keep each year picture God's great plan for mankind.

This lesson will explain the meaning of the spring festivals. They are the Passover, the Days of Unleavened Bread and Pentecost. These festivals picture the first three steps in God's plan.

THE PASSOVER

Thousands of years ago, the Israelite people were **slaves** in Egypt. They spent many long years of suffering from hard work, until God chose a man named Moses to free them.

God told Moses to go to the Pharaoh, king of Egypt, and ask him to let the Israelites go free. Each time Moses asked, Pharaoh said, "No!" God would then send a terrible **plague** on the people of Egypt. This happened nine times. But one more plague was to come. Let's look at the last plague, because it has much to do with the first Passover and Pharaoh's freeing of the Israelites (Exodus 11 and 12 tell us about it).

Parents: Explain the words in **boldface**. Explain "slaves" so your child will understand why the Israelites wanted to be free. Also explain "plague," and review the other plagues the Egyptians suffered.

The tenth and last plague God sent was the death of the firstborn in the land of Egypt. This included the death of the firstborn animals as well as the people. If you are the oldest child in your family, you are the firstborn.

God told the Israelites that on the night of the Passover they were to roast a healthy male lamb and eat it with their families. They were to eat it with unleavened bread and bitter herbs. They were told to take some of the blood of the lamb and smear it on the doorposts of their houses. God's angel would see the blood and **pass over** their houses, sparing their firstborn from death. Then they were also told to eat flat or unleavened bread for seven days.

God commanded that the Passover be kept every year from that time forward. When Christ came to this earth, He changed the way it was to be kept.

Today, on Passover night your parents attend a special church service. They wash the feet of other members, which shows a humble and serving attitude. Then they eat a piece of unleavened bread. The bread is a reminder that Christ's body was horribly beaten before He died so that we could be healed when we are sick. Your parents then drink a glass of wine which pictures the blood that poured out of Christ's body. He died so that we could be forgiven of our sins.

THE DAYS OF UNLEAVENED BREAD

The second festival in God's plan is the Days of Unleavened Bread. We keep this feast by not eating anything with leavening in it for seven days. God tells us to have all leavening out of our homes during this time. This is why just before these days, your

---

Parents: Explain what you do on Passover night. Be sure to include the significance of the foot washing, unleavened bread and wine.

mother cleans the cupboards and pantry and throws out all the crackers, cookies, and any other foods which contain leavening.

The lesson God wants to teach us by this festival is to put sin or wrong-doing out of our lives just as we put out the leavening. Remember that leaven puffs things up just as sin puffs us up. For this reason, God wants us to put away sin or doing wrong before it spreads to other areas of our lives.

God wants us to keep His Commandments. Eating unleavened bread for seven days reminds us of this lesson and our need to obey Him. This year as you help your mother put out this leavening, remember the lesson God wants us to learn from this festival.

PENTECOST

Let's now take a look at the third festival picturing the third step in God's plan. It is called Pentecost, and means "fiftieth (day)." Pentecost is fifty days from (beginning with) the Sunday after the Sabbath which usually comes during the Days of Unleavened Bread. Another name for Pentecost is the "Feast of Firstfruits." Pentecost pictures the Church today and how it fits into God's plan.

Many years ago, Jesus Christ came to earth and died on Passover day. He was then resurrected, or made alive, after being dead three days and three nights. He then went to heaven to appear before God the Father. Fifty days later, God sent the Holy Spirit to Christ's disciples on the Day of Pentecost.

The Holy Spirit is a special spiritual help which God gives to those who have been baptized. Before you receive the Holy

---

Parents: Explain more about God's way of "give," contrasting it with Satan's way of "get." Tell your child the importance of sharing his or her toys so others, too, can receive enjoyment. Explain why it is important to have a serving attitude.

Spirit, you only have the "spirit in man" which makes you very different from the animals because it makes it possible for you to think and reason. Because you are children of baptized parents, you have the Holy Spirit working **with** you, but when you are baptized (when you are grown up) you will have the Holy Spirit **in** your mind to help you do what is right.

The Day of Pentecost shows us that the people in God's Church who have received His Holy Spirit are the "firstfruits" of all those to be called by God to understand His ways and be born into His Family. The "firstfruits" are the ones who will help Christ teach God's way of life to the rest of mankind in the World Tomorrow. Since no human but Christ has yet been given eternal life, Christ is the **first** of the firstfruits to be born into the Family of God.

The people in God's Church are the first to be given the opportunity to become members of God's Family. Later, when Christ returns to earth and sets up His ruling Kingdom, the entire world will be given the opportunity. This includes all those who have lived and died, but have never heard or understood this wonderful truth of God!

The festivals of the Passover, Days of Unleavened Bread, and Pentecost teach us the first three steps in God's plan for mankind. In the special Fall Festival Lesson, you will learn the meaning of the last four steps in God's plan, as pictured by the four feasts which come in the fall.

Parents: Explain how the Holy Spirit that is with your children can be a benefit if they ask God for help.

The Israelite fathers prepared a lamb for the Passover. They smeared blood on their doorposts, so the death angel would **pass over** and not kill their firstborn.

Parents: Explain to your child that just as God protected the Israelites who obeyed Him that first Passover, God also protects His people who obey Him today.

Today, these are the things God's people do on Passover night to remember Christ's death.

Parents: Instruct your child to color the pictures. Also, review the meaning of Passover, and the meaning of each of the pictures.

The Israelites were very happy that God delivered them from slavery in Egypt!

Parents: Ask your child this question: What did the Israelites celebrate on the night they left Egypt, that God's people celebrate today?

Just before the Days of Unleavened Bread, we must put all the leavening out of our homes.

Parents: Ask your child what leavening has to do with bread. Then explain the relationship between leavening and sin, and why it is so important not to sin.

Pentecost pictures God's people as the "firstfruits" of those he is calling into his Family.

Parents: Explain to your child that he or she will help teach God's way of life—the way of "give"—in the world tomorrow.

MY SCRAPBOOK

Parents: Your child may wish to paste photographs
of the Night to Be Much Observed here.

Originally published by the Worldwide Church of God
Produced in cooperation with Imperial Schools
Copyright© 1981. Reprint by *Continuing* Church of God • www.ccog.org

BIBLE MEMORY

Parents: Have your child circle the items they are NOT to eat during the Days of Unleavened Bread.

Made in the USA
Columbia, SC
10 August 2019